Charles Edward Barrett-Lennard

**Travels in British Columbia**

With the Narrative of a Yacht Voyage round Vancouver's Island

Charles Edward Barrett-Lennard

**Travels in British Columbia**
*With the Narrative of a Yacht Voyage round Vancouver's Island*

ISBN/EAN: 9783337212698

Printed in Europe, USA, Canada, Australia, Japan

Cover: Foto ©Andreas Hilbeck / pixelio.de

More available books at **www.hansebooks.com**

EX LIBRIS
ROBERT GIBSON

VICTORIA FROM JAMES' BAY, LOOKING UP GOVERNMENT STREET.

*From a Photograph by Lt. Richard Roche.*

# TRAVELS IN BRITISH COLUMBIA,

WITH THE NARRATIVE

OF

# A YACHT VOYAGE

ROUND

VANCOUVER'S ISLAND.

BY

CAPT. C. E. BARRETT-LENNARD.

IN ONE VOLUME.

LONDON:
HURST AND BLACKETT, PUBLISHERS.
SUCCESSORS TO HENRY COLBURN,
13, GREAT MARLBOROUGH STREET.
1862.

*The right of Translation is reserved.*

LONDON:
PRINTED BY R. BORN, GLOUCESTER STREET,
REGENT'S PARK.

# PREFACE.

THE interest which at the present moment attaches to everything connected with British Columbia and Vancouver's Island, has induced me to believe that a narrative of personal adventure and experience in these still comparatively unknown but highly important colonies might prove not only acceptable to the general reader, but of practical utility to the intending emigrant.

Having spent two years on the Pacific coast of the North American continent, and having, in addition to numerous land excursions, passed a considerable time cruising in a yacht round the Island of Vancouver, I have enjoyed unusual opportunities of becoming acquainted not only with the general physical character and geographical features of the country, but also with the habits and customs of the different Indian tribes here located. I can, moreover, assure my readers that such information as I have to offer is of the most recent date; a fact of no small importance in connection with colonies where everything is undergoing a most rapid transformation, where flourishing townships and settlements are daily springing up in districts which a few years back were covered with forests of primeval pine.

*Royal Thames Yacht Club, London,*
*Aug., 1862.*

# CONTENTS.

### CHAPTER I.

Principal Routes from England to British Columbia and Vancouver's Island—Panama Route. Cape Horn Route—Voyage out—Difficulty of rounding Cape Horn—Contrary Winds and Heavy Seas—Inclemency of the Weather—We sight Cape Horn—Valparaiso—Change from Cold to Heat—Fine Run on leaving Valparaiso—Termination of the Voyage—Straits of Juan de Fuca—Size of Vancouver's Island—General Description—Pine Woods—Indian Paths or Trails through the Interior—Appearance of the Coast—Climate of Vancouver's Island and British Columbia—Natural Productions—Wild Animals—Fish—Channel between Vancouver's Island and the Mainland—Varying Depth of Water—Tides—Floating Timber—Kelp . . . . 1

### CHAPTER II.

British Columbia—Fraser River—First Discoverers—Drake—Captain Cook—Vancouver—Town of Victoria—When Founded—Governor Douglas—Harbour of Victoria—Esquimalt—Mail Steamers—Post Office—Wells, Fargo, and Co.—Rapid Improvement of Victoria — First Impressions — Indian Village and Burial Ground—Character of Surrounding Country—Picturesque Scenery . . . . . . . . 19

### CHAPTER III.

Departure on our Cruise—A Night on the Island of San Juan—Depth of Water—Point Roberts—Fraser River—New Westminster, Capital of British Columbia—Head-quarters of the Royal Engineers—" The Brunette "—Enormous Timber—Strong Current—Nanaimo—Coal on Vancouver's Island—A Hunting Expedition—Leave Nanaimo—Uculta Village—Valdez Island—Stiff Breeze—Dangerous Reef of Rocks—Fort Rupert . . 27

## CONTENTS.

### CHAPTER IV.

Indian Tribes inhabiting Vancouver's Island—Northern Indians visiting the Island periodically—Enmity among the Different Tribes—Indian Warfare—Weapons—Canoes—Treachery of the Ucultas—General Appearance of the Indians—Artificial Flattening of the Skull—Use of Paint—Indian Women—Dress—Indian Village—Huts—Fishing Season—Salmon—Articles of Food—Whisky—Carving—Construction of Canoe—Indian Burial-Ground—Mysteries of the Kluquolla—Gambling—Indian Superstitions . . . . . . . . . 39

### CHAPTER V.

Indian Servants—Mode of Dealing with Indians—Misconduct of the Hydahs—They fire on the "Rob Roy"—Prompt Measures taken by the Authorities to Redress the Outrage—The Hydahs are brought to Reason—Captain John—His Capture and Death—Adventure of the Cowichin Indian—Northern Marauders—Lieutenant Robson sets out in Pursuit—Insolent Defiance of the Indians—Effect of the Great Guns—The Ucultas—Fort Rupert—Excellent Garden—Kindness of the Chief Factor—We leave Fort Rupert—Round the North-west Point of the Island—Carried by the Tide past our Destination—Quatsinough Harbour—Koshkeemo Village—Our Indian Host—The Interior of a Hut—Domestic Life—Indian Apathy . . 59

### CHAPTER VI.

Weather changes for the worse—Heavy Rains—Time consumed by Indians in striking a Bargain—Religious Chants—Ancient Carvings—Salmon Weir—We leave our Anchorage—Heavy Swell at Sea—Dangerous Rocks—Difficult and Hazardous Navigation—Bay of Klaskeeno—Cogwell Trader—Want of Fresh Food—Klaskeeno River—Contrary Winds—Critical Position of our Yacht—Assistance rendered by Indians—Fresh Ballast on Board—Improvement in the Weather—We again put to Sea . . . 78

## CHAPTER VII.

Heavy Seas after Recent Gales—Freshsets from the Coast—Mocuina Point—Escalante Reef—We drift out to Sea—Thick Fog—Make Friendly Cove—Nootka Sound—Strange Sail on the Horizon—Indians come alongside—Cooptee, Winter Quarters of the Mowichats—Noise made over a Kluquolla—Mocoola, Chief of the Mowichats—Takes a Fancy to our Dog—Indian Opinion of European Garments—Pe-Sha-Klim, Spouter of the Mowichats—Indian Presents—Tomahawk and other Arms—Narrative of an Adventure on our Former Visit—We ascend Guaquina Arm—Hostility of the Matchelats—Indian Warwhoop—They fire on us—We parley with them—Peace Restored—We go on Shore with the Chief—Encampment—Fresh Symptoms of Hostility—Satisfactory Explanations—Fail to reach the Object of our Expedition—Arrival of Pe-Sha-Klim . . . . . . . . . 91

## CHAPTER VIII.

The Wreck of the "Florentia"—Sufferings of the Crew—Resolution Cove—Perilous Adventure in an Open Boat—Bocca del Inferno—Misunderstanding between the Shipwrecked Crew and the Indians—Dress of an Indian Woman—The Use of Paint—Primitive *Poste-Restante*—Captain Cook . . . . 111

## CHAPTER IX.

We leave Nootka Sound—Variable Winds—Bajo Reef—We part our Cable—A Favourable Wind—Our Prospects brighten—We fail to make Clayoquot Sound—Our Former Visit—Summer Village of the Clayoquot Indians—Their Warlike Character—Murder of Esquibat Chief—Narrow Escape of a White Man—A Battle in Canoes—Midnight Attack—We re-enter Juan de Fuca Straits—Return to Victoria—Christmas in Vancouver's Island—General Improvements . . . . . 123

## CHAPTER X.

We revisit British Columbia—The Fraser River and Gold-Fields—New Westminster—The Harrison Lillooett Route described—Skaholet Indians—Harrison River and Lake—Port Douglas—Encampment of Royal Engineers—Strong Current—Chinese Gold-Seekers—Fort Hope—Romantic Scenery—Tum Sioux Indians—Religious Ceremony—"Tumanas," or "Medicine Man"—Route from Fort Hope to Lillooett, on the way to Cariboo . . . . . . . . . 139

## CHAPTER XI.

General Remarks on British Columbia—Its Soil and Climate—Agricultural Prospects—Its Natural Productions—Mineral, Vegetable, and Animal—Suitability of its Climate to rearing English Stock—Encouragement to Farmers to settle here—The Gold Fields—Prospects of Miners—Advice to Gold Seekers—A Miner's Narrative—Different Methods of seeking for Gold—Other Branches of Industry—Packers—Effect of the Discovery of Gold on British Columbia—Geographical Features of the Country—Its Mountains, Rivers, and Lakes . . . . . . 153

## CHAPTER XII.

Idea of an Inter-Oceanic Line of Railway—United States Line—Importance of such a Line of Railroad on British Territory—Circumstances favouring its Adoption—Great Advantages attending it—The Splendid Future it would open to British Columbia and Vancouver's Island—The Overland Route from St. Paul's, Minnesota, to British Columbia, by the Red River and Saskatchewan—Its Practicability discussed—The Country through which it passes—Probable Expense of the Journey—Routes followed by Mr. M'Laurin, in 1858 and 1860—Recent Accounts of Canadians about to undertake the Journey—Difficulties of crossing the Rocky Mountains—Letters in the "Times"—Company recently started for conveying Emigrants by this Route . . . . . . 178

CONTENTS. xi

CHAPTER XIII.

New Routes through the Interior of British Columbia—The Bentinck Arm Route—The Bute Inlet Route—Effect of opening up New Routes to Cariboo—Gold on the Stickeen River—Gold on the North and Tranquille Rivers—Gold on the Upper Columbia River—Importance of opening a Route through British Territory—Captain Venables on the Bill-Whoalla Route—Route through American Territory—Probable Rush to the Gold Fields of British Columbia from California—Diggings on the Salmon River—A Sketch of the Journey across North America, as formerly accomplished . . . . . . . 205

CHAPTER XIV.

We leave Victoria for San Francisco—Wells Fargo's Agency—The Mirage—A Modern "Robinson Crusoe"—Yankee Habits—Columbia River—Portland—We strike on a Rock—The Water gains on us in spite of all our Efforts—Critical Situation of the Steamer "Pacific"—We run her ashore—Portland—Picturesque Scenery on the Columbia River—San Francisco—Its Harbour—Description of the Town—Mexican Drovers—The Firemen of San Francisco—Effect of the Gold-Fever—Japanese Embassy—American Driving—Race-course—American Opinion of a Fox-Hunt—The "General" Drinking Bars—Theatres—Union Club—The "Pony Express"—The Chinese in San Francisco—The Vigilance Committee . 224

CHAPTER XV.

Departure from San Francisco—Benicia—Sacramento City—Its Situation—Natural Productions of California—Row in the House of Assembly—Use of the Revolver and Knife—Opinion of an American on American Institutions—Probable Effects of the Present War in the United States—Its Causes—Tariff to protect the Manufacturing Interests—Hatred between the North and South—Results to be anticipated at the Close of the

# TRAVELS IN BRITISH COLUMBIA.

## CHAPTER I.

Principal Routes from England to British Columbia and Vancouver's Island—Panama Route. Cape Horn Route—Voyage out—Difficulty of Rounding Cape Horn—Contrary Winds and Heavy Seas —Inclemency of the Weather—We sight Cape Horn—Valparaiso—Change from Cold to Heat—Fine Run on leaving Valparaiso—Termination of the Voyage—Straits of Juan de Fuca— Size of Vancouver's Island—General Description—Pine Woods— Indian Paths or Trails through the Interior—Appearance of the Coast—Climate of Vancouver's Island and British Columbia— Natural Productions—Wild Animals—Fish—Channel between Vancouver's Island and the Mainland—Varying Depth of Water—Tides—Floating Timber—Kelp.

INTENDING emigrants and visitors to British Columbia and Vancouver's Island have at present the choice of two routes, the ordinary one by sea, *via* Cape Horn, which involves a sea voyage of some 20,000 miles, and the so-called overland route, *via* Panama, whereby the distance and duration of the voyage are greatly abridged. Of the true overland route from New York to St. Joseph's,

Missouri, by rail, and thence to California and the Pacific, by stage coaches, passing the Mormon city of Utah, I shall have occasion to speak hereafter. One of the chief objections to the Panama route, however, consists in the possible delay which may occur at Panama through waiting for the arrival of the steamer from San Francisco, which, in a climate so extremely unhealthy, may be attended with serious consequences. I would impress on any one, whose fate it may be to be thus detained, never to expose himself to the poisonous exhalations of the district after nightfall.

The Panama route may be diversified by going in the first instance direct to New York, whence steamers sail twice a week to the former place.

The railroad across the Isthmus of Panama, connecting the Pacific with the Gulf of Mexico and the Atlantic, is a Yankee speculation which has been justly characterized as a work resting on a foundation of human bones, having cost the lives of thousands of the Irish navvies employed in its construction. The transit occupies about three hours from Aspinwall to the old Spanish port of Panama, and the line of rail runs through a dense tropical growth of luxuriant vegetation.

The other route round Cape Horn, the so-called sea-route, involves a journey of some five or six months' duration; consequently, every requisite for a long voyage should be provided by those who adopt it; they should, moreover, bear in mind that the extremes of latitude they will have to traverse are sufficiently great to cause a double alternation of winter and summer during the voyage. Ere they reach Cape Horn they will have exchanged the North Star for the Southern Cross, and long before they arrive at their destination, after having doubled that Cape of Storms, the Southern Cross will have disappeared below the horizon, and their old acquaintance the North Star will again be high in the heavens. We would therefore advise every one, intending to take this route, to provide himself with a wardrobe sufficiently varied to meet the exigencies of tropical heat and almost Arctic cold.

I see that steamers have recently been advertised to sail from England by this route to British Columbia. This will prove a great boon to intending emigrants, as not only will the duration of the voyage be abridged by the increased speed of the mode of conveyance, but its actual length will be considerably diminished by enabling them to make their passage through the Straits of Magellan, thereby also avoiding the dangerous storms and icebergs round Cape Horn.

That the reader may be able to form some idea of the experiences of a long sea voyage, I will briefly detain him while I give him a sketch of our own. We left the Downs in the month of September,

1859, and, after a fine run, found ourselves off the Island of Madeira—the weather deliciously balmy. We crossed the line on the 20th October, with the thermometer, perhaps, 120° on deck, one day, followed by a perfect deluge of rain on the next, when it was quite a luxury to get thoroughly wet through. Shortly after crossing the line the monotony of our voyage was agreeably diversified by speaking a vessel bound for London, thus giving us an opportunity of sending our friends at home some tidings of our whereabouts in the realms of old Neptune.

We lay-to for a couple of days, off the river Plate, in something very like a gale of wind—the first really bad weather we had hitherto experienced.

In a short time, however, the skies were again propitious, and we remember, about this time, running through the midst of a fleet of whalers, while a few days later we first smelt the land, as it is technically termed, some considerable time, however, before it was actually visible. This singular phenomenon is well known to seamen, and even animals on board ship testify to their consciousness of it by unusual excitement. A favourable breeze springing up from the E. and N.E. sent us on our way rejoicing, through the Straits of Lemaire, between the Falkland Islands and the mainland of South America. Some vessels touch at this group of islands on their passage out. Indeed, their so doing may happen to be compulsory, through stress of weather, and it is not unfrequently the fate of the unhappy voyager in these tempestuous seas to sight these islands periodically, for weeks together, when detained by adverse winds. One of the chief objections against the route round Cape Horn lies in the fact that the winds blow constantly, for nine months in the year, from the westward, directly in the teeth therefore of outward-bound vessels, but rendering it, at the same time, a very desirable route for the passage home. This is the reason why vessels from Australia to England return round Cape Horn. As for ourselves, we must confess that we had no special grounds for dissatisfaction, as we were not detained more than three weeks on this part of our passage. It was also our fate to pass much closer to the actual shore of the island than is usually the case, so close, indeed, that we were enabled to obtain a distinct view of Cape Horn itself, the most southernly point of these wild, rugged, and inclement regions.

To continue my narrative, however, we found ourselves, after running through the Straits of Lemaire, off Statten Island, one Sunday morning, the weather growing rapidly colder. Steering in a westernly direction, we doubled Cape St. John, with its castle-like rocks, the home of innumerable sea-birds of every description.

After sighting the extreme point of Cape Horn, in the middle of November, distant at the time about five miles, we were compelled to run down as far to southward as latitude 60°, to enable us to beat sufficiently to the westward to clear the southernmost extremity of the great American continent.

We experienced the usual gales which fall to the lot of all voyagers outward-bound who attempt to double this " Cape of Storms," a name it deserves certainly in a greater degree than even the Cape of Good Hope itself. As far as our experience goes, there is no part of the world in which heavier seas may be expected than in these latitudes; and the aspect presented on one or two occasions by the ocean, as we beheld it from the deck of our vessel, was such as no landsman who saw it would ever be likely to forget. There is something exceedingly wild and desolate in the appearance of both sky and sea during a gale of wind in these latitudes—a driving rain or sleet beat unceasingly in our faces, as our vessel plunged and rolled among the monstrous waves, till she showed the whole of her copper sheathing on one side, or dipped the end of her yard-arm into the boiling ocean on the other; now buried in the hollow between two rolling ridges of water, now rising with a sudden heave to the giant swell as it swept beneath her, while its bursting crest of foam deluged our decks with water, and sent the spray flying in clouds through our rigging.

When in latitude 60° south, the region of keen winds and icebergs, of fur coats, warm wraps, and red noses, we found the cold sufficiently severe, although near Midsummer, to be very unpleasant—what it may be in winter, when innumerable icebergs add to the terrors of the scene, we have no desire to experience. We contrived, however, to amuse ourselves on one or two occasions by knocking over an albatross or a Cape fowl, both of which are sufficiently difficult shooting.

After being baffled for some time by contrary winds and thick foggy weather—with driving rain and sudden squalls, to which these regions are very subject—during which time we never caught sight of the sun, and were, therefore, unable to form a correct idea of our whereabouts, we at length got a glimpse of the luminary of day, which enabled us to verify both our latitude and longitude, and led us to hope that the worst of our voyage was over.

At the same time I repeat that we have no reason to complain of having experienced unusually harsh treatment in these inhospitable seas, and future travellers may thank their stars if they escape as well as we did. After having fairly doubled Cape Horn, favourable winds soon carried us into warmer latitudes, and our winter clothing was exchanged for light summer garments ere we reached Valparaiso, the chief port of entry on the Coast of Chile. Here we were as pleased as a parcel of schoolboys turned out for a holiday, to get a scamper on shore.

The town of Valparaiso stands on the shores of a bay forming a natural harbour, at the entrance to which a good light-house has been erected. The British Government maintains a store-ship here for the use of the Royal Navy. The appearance of the town is not particularly striking, the majority of the houses being built of wood or iron; the warehouses are, however, very handsome buildings. As it was the 26th of December when we landed—the Midsummer of these latitudes—the place had a very dry, hot, and dusty look, and the heat was in reality quite as great as we cared about, even after the cold winds of Cape Horn. A further acquaintance with the place revealed to us several buildings of a more substantial character, as well as some neat suburban residences on the sides of the hills in its vicinity. There are a great number of foreign residents in the place, the trade being chiefly in the hands of English and French merchants; and as a proof of the normally unsettled condition of politics in those regions, I may mention that every house has a flagstaff on its roof, in order that its owner may display the flag of his nation, and thus claim immunity from attack, in the event of any sudden popular outburst or revolution. The town of Valparaiso is enclosed in an amphitheatre of hills, and from the harbour may be obtained a fine view of the distant Andes. I cannot take leave of this place without recording an indignant protest against the inefficiency of its postal arrangements. Notwithstanding the kindness of the consul, who spared no trouble on my behalf, I was unable to obtain several letters and papers, which I knew ought to have been awaiting me here; nor could I hear anything of them when I wrote for them months afterwards from Vancouver, although backed by the influence of two consuls.

A day or two after leaving Valparaiso, the breeze that took us out carried us well into the zone of the south-east trade winds, and we had the good fortune to make a run of some 4,000 miles on our course, almost without having occasion to trim our sails. This was succeeded by contrary and uncertain winds, which continued for some time to baffle and delay our course. At length, to the delight of all on board, we sighted the light on Cape Classet, which heralded the termination of our lengthened cruise.

After being some hours balked by an adverse wind, we at length found ourselves fairly in the Straits of Juan de Fuca, and next morning, after a pouring wet night, were within sight of the Race Rocks, on which a lighthouse has recently been erected. Two hours after we had passed them we took our pilot on board. The narrow entrance to the Harbour of Victoria itself, however, only revealed itself at the very last moment.

Before actually setting foot on shore, and introducing my readers to the little wooden town of Victoria, as it then appeared, I propose giving them some idea of the general character, natural features, and climate of the country I have undertaken to describe.

The island of Vancouver itself—in length about 250 miles, with an extreme breadth of 70—is separated from the mainland by the Straits of Juan de Fuca, the Gulf of Georgia, Johnson's Straits, and Queen Charlotte's Sound.

As far as my observations up to the present moment would lead me to conclude, this large island is one vast rock, in most places but thinly covered with a virgin soil, the result of vegetable decay, highly productive wherever it is to be met with of sufficient depth. The island is traversed, apparently throughout its entire length, by a ridge of pine-covered mountains, of varied elevation, rising, however, in many places to a very considerable altitude. Having thus alluded to the pine, the staple natural production of the country, I may describe Vancouver's Island as one vast forest of thickly-grown pine. These primeval forests of sombre green give a somewhat gloomy character to the scenery of this part of the world. Let not the European reader imagine, however, that these forests are like anything which he may have seen in the Old World. With the exception of an occasional Indian trail, these woods are, owing to the thick, jungle-like undergrowth, wholly impenetrable. The trees composing them are forced up to an immense height, and are, as a natural consequence, remarkably straight and upright in their growth, even when of gigantic girth, furnishing, in fact, some of the noblest spars in the universe. I am glad to find that the British public are likely to have an opportunity of forming some idea of the magnitude of these vegetable Goliaths from an actual specimen proposed to be set up, as I am given to understand, at Kensington Gore. A section of one of the stems may also be seen in the part of the International Exhibition appropriated to the productions of Vancouver's Island.

I may here take occasion to observe, in connection with these forests, that a vast conflagration 'will from time to time break out in the midst of their very densest portions, arising, it has been conjectured, from the spontaneous combustion of accumulated masses of decayed vegetation. Whatever be the cause of them, certain it is that these fires are continually occurring. I have frequently beheld them myself, and their result is to give a most desolate and even frightful appearance to the district in which they occur. I have seen, whilst sailing near the shore, vast spaces, many square miles in extent, entirely denuded of anything like vegetation—converted, in fact, into a wilderness of scorched and blackened ashes, in the midst of which the gaunt, charred stems of the former monarchs of the forest stand. at intervals, like sentinel mourners over the graves of their kindred.

In speaking of Vancouver as one vast forest of pine, I give the result of my own observation— such, with the occasional patches of cleared and cultivated land, it has always appeared to me, from whatever point of view it has been my lot to behold it. At the same time I feel bound to mention that the Indians persist in stating that extensive open plains exist in the interior, and that there is a water communication, by means of a chain of lake and river, from Nittinat, Barclay Sound, on the south-west coast, to the village of the Nimkish Indians, at the mouth of the Nimkish river, flowing into Johnson's Straits, on the northeast side of the island, within thirty miles, by sea, of Fort Rupert. How far this assertion of the Indians will be verified by future research, remains to be proved; that a communication, also chiefly by water, does actually exist between the village of the Nimkish Indians and Nootka Sound is a well-known fact—this runs through the centre of the island, and has probably been used by the Hudson's Bay traders. One other means of communication across the island exists between

Nanaimo, the coaling station on the Gulf of Georgia, and the new settlement on Alberni canal, Barclay Sound, Pacific.

From the foregoing description of the island, my readers will, no doubt, be prepared to hear that the coast of Vancouver is rocky and abrupt; it is, moreover, on all sides, surrounded by an infinite number of rocky islets. These, on the Pacific coast, are mere naked rocks, but in the channel we meet with habitable islands many square miles in extent.

As the latitude of Vancouver, lying between 48° and 52° N., corresponds with that of a portion of Canada, on the opposite side of the North American continent, we might naturally be prepared to meet with something like a corresponding vigour of climate. In this, however, we shall be agreeably disappointed. The climate of the Pacific coast of this continent, is infinitely milder and more genial than that of corresponding districts on the Atlantic coast. How this fact is to be accounted for on natural grounds—whether any inter-tropical ocean current, flowing along this coast, performs the same good office for it that the Gulf Stream is supposed to do for us—I leave to *savans* to determine; suffice it to say that the extremes of cold and heat are seldom felt to be at all inconvenient, and there are, I apprehend, few parts of the world in which the Englishman will find a climate more resembling his own, even to the amount of rain that may be expected to fall in the year. There is one fact, however, to which I would direct special attention, as it may be important to the intending emigrant; it is this—however warm the day, after nightfall, a cold wind is sure to set in from the adjacent continent, which, coming as it does from the snow-covered Alps of that region, is very keen and penetrating. I may here, indeed, take occasion to remark that the extremes of heat and cold will be found to be greater as we advance into the interior of the continent. As might be expected in such a climate, most of the vegetable productions of the British Islands may here be successfully cultivated. The wild growth of the island is prolific in berries of every description. Among these we shall recognize several old acquaintances, and none with more pleasure than the fragrant strawberry of our native woodlands.

The fauna of this region is varied and important, at the same time I cannot promise the sportsman so abundant a field for the exercise of his skill as might be anticipated, on account of the impenetrable nature of the woods. Birds, however, of all descriptions, are everywhere to be met with on the coasts. Among the larger and more formidable of the wild animals, I may mention the bear, the panther, and the wolf. The former is the well-known black bear of the North American continent; both the latter are animals possessing the usual characteristics of their tribe. Deer, of large size, and graced with noble antlers, are common. The way in which they take the water in their migrations from the mainland, or from one island to another, is very noticeable; they think nothing of crossing an arm of the sea, and we have been credibly informed that they have been met with several miles from land. Their flesh is capital venison. Many of the more valued furs are the produce of animals abounding in Vancouver, while, as I before remarked, birds of all descriptions are very plentiful; among them we may enumerate the wild goose, ducks of various species, the blue grouse, the heron, and innumerable flocks of sea birds. Most of the rivers and streams are full of fish, among which we shall meet with many old favourites. Both trout and salmon are abundant, and of excellent quality, and I can speak in the highest terms of the flavour of the native prawn; the oysters also are said to be good. Neither the lobster nor the crab is, however, to be met with; nor do I consider their absence compensated for by the existing kinds of shell-fish. The noted clam, so highly prized in America, is here very abundant.

I have already had occasion to speak several times of the channel separating the island of Vancouver from the mainland. This possesses natural features of a sufficiently marked and interesting character to merit a special notice. Its length is about 340 miles, while its width varies from two or three to thirty miles; a great portion of it is filled with islands of all sizes, as I have already stated, together with sunken rocks. As might be supposed, in a sea of this description, the results obtained by sounding are very various, but the reader will probably hardly be prepared to hear that the extraordinary depth of seventy or eighty fathoms is frequently met with, and this, in many cases, under the very shadow of the rocky coast of the island itself. I remember on one occasion a sounding, taken at our bow, gave a depth of eight fathoms, while that at our stern gave fifteen; and on another we obtained eight, and sixty fathoms, as the result of two successive throws of our line. Again, no reliable theory has yet been arrived at, with regard to the ebb and flow of the tides, in this singular and capricious sea. I do not overstate their fitful character, when I say they are as little to be depended on as the winds themselves, seeming, indeed, to be governed by none of the known and recognized laws of tidal action. It is no uncommon thing for the tide to ebb for three hours, and flow for eighteen. These wild and lawless currents, setting in from the ocean, through the opposite extremities of the channel, meet in its narrowest portion, called Johnson's Straits, characteristically known as the Rapids. The absolute point of meeting is, as far as I was able to form an opinion, opposite Cape Mudge, at the southern extremity of Valdez Island, forming a series of eddies and whirlpools, locally known as tide-rips, in which a vessel is carried helplessly along, unless a very strong breeze is blowing. The navigation of these narrow seas is, moreover, much impeded by floating timber, of gigantic proportions, and also by enormous beds of that extraordinary marine plant, the kelp. I have seen a vessel of forty or fifty tons, with a fair breeze, brought up dead, as if at anchor, by coming suddenly on a bed of kelp, and woe betide the hapless wight whose fate it may be to get entangled, while bathing, among the treacherous rope-like stems, and long, leathery leaves of this Brobdignag, submarine growth: he is caught, like a fly, in the meshes of a spider, and with as little chance of escape. To this fact I can testify, from several painful cases of brave fellows and capital swimmers who thus lost their lives during my stay in the colony.

One other natural peculiarity is noticeable in the waters of this channel. I allude to their extreme coldness. So great indeed did I find this, that in bathing I seldom had courage to venture beyond my depth. The description I have given of the shores of the island applies equally, in its leading characteristics, to the general appearance of the mainland; here also the shores are covered down to the water's edge with dense forests of pine; the open spaces, whether natural or artificially cleared, being only met with at rare intervals, during clear weather, a range of lofty mountains may be distinguished in the distance, many of them rising to the altitude of snow-covered Alps.

## CHAPTER II.

British Columbia—Fraser River—First Discoverers—Drake—Captain Cook—Vancouver—Town of Victoria—When Founded—Governor Douglas—Harbour of Victoria—Esquimalt—Mail Steamers—Post Office—Wells, Fargo, and Co.—Rapid Improvement of Victoria—First Impressions—Indian Village and Burial Ground—Character of Surrounding Country—Picturesque Scenery.

THE town of Victoria, capital of Vancouver's Island, was originally a station or port of the Hudson's Bay Company, founded in 1843, and, like everything else in this part of the world, is of recent date. It was in pursuit of their arduous and venturesome calling that the Hudson's Bay fur traders first visited this "Ultima Thule" of the West, crossing the channel that separates it from the mainland. The name British Columbia is quite a modern term; the original appellation bestowed upon it by Captain Cook being New

Caledonia. The territory now known as British Columbia is situated entirely on the mainland or continent of North America, and is bounded on the north by Simpson's River, on the south by the United States Territory, east by the Rocky Mountains, and west by the Pacific; being separated from the Island of Vancouver by Juan de Fuca Straits, the Gulf of Georgia, Johnson's Straits, and Queen Charlotte's Sound. Its length is upwards of 400 miles, and its average width 300.

The first settlers on the now world-famous Fraser's River date from the year 1806 only, about which time that auriferous stream—the modern Phasis—received its present appellation. It takes its rise in the Rocky Mountains, the great central chain of North America, whence it flows, in its course to the Gulf of Georgia, through the gold-producing district of Cariboo. It is, we think, certain that the original discoverers of the American Continent, the Spaniards, never penetrated thus far. There is, however, no doubt, that Queen Elizabeth indignantly protested against the arrogant pretensions of the Spanish King, who, in virtue of a Papal Bull, laid claim to these and other territories on the coast of the Pacific. This protest was followed by an expedition, fitted out under command of the gallant Drake, to assert that supremacy on the seas which his country has ever since maintained, and will maintain in spite of all the Papal Bulls that ever issued from the Vatican. Drake, undoubtedly, reached the territory of British Columbia, and gave it the name of New Albion. The example of Drake was followed by Cavendish, and shortly afterwards by Juan de Fuca, whose name is borne by the Straits to the south of Vancouver. Notwithstanding this fact, however, doubts have been expressed as to whether any navigator of this name really existed or not. Among the more modern explorers of these regions, I may mention the name of the unfortunate Behring, who, crossing over to the American continent from Kamschatka, discovered Mount Elias, and eventually perished on the island which still bears his name. We now come to the period of the voyages of the celebrated Captain Cook, of whose visit to these shores some of the Indian tribes still preserve traditions. To him belongs the credit of having first thoroughly explored the coast-line of British Columbia and Vancouver. The number of fur-bearing animals he discovered in these territories naturally attracted the attention of the Russians, as great consumers of fur, and the result was the acquisition by their Government of the line of coast known as Russian America. It was the pursuit of similar objects, on the part of the United States, that led to the long debated question of disputed boundary, known as the Oregon question. The insular character of

Vancouver was first demonstrated by the navigator whose name it bears, and who sailed round it in 1792.

The town of Victoria may, in its origin, be regarded as the last link in that wonderful chain of stations or forts extending completely across the American continent, which owe their existence to the undaunted energy, enterprise, and perseverance of the gallant traders of the Hudson's Bay Company, a body of men of whom any country might be proud, who, in the teeth of hardships and dangers of every description have thus been the pioneers of civilization, through the heart of this mighty continent. The old Hudson's Bay Fort of Victoria was situated in the district occupied by the aboriginal tribe of the Songees. They, however, parted with their claim to the company, and migrated to the other side of the harbour. The island of Vancouver was granted to the Hudson's Bay Company, on condition of their colonizing it in 1848. James Douglas, the present Governor, was the chief factor of this company at Fort Victoria, and when the natural resources of the country, developed by increased immigration, entitled it to be erected into one of the colonies of the British Empire, he was, on account of his extensive experience and knowledge of the country, as well as the influence he wielded in the colony, selected for the post of Governor.

## ESQUIMALT. 23

The harbour of Victoria is of irregular form, consisting of two basins, of which the inner one constitutes the real harbour. This may be entered at high water by vessels of considerable tonnage, which can then lie alongside the wharves of Victoria. The rocks in the outer harbour form some impediment to navigation, which is nevertheless readily overcome by a skilful pilot. To state my real convictions, however, I believe that the harbour of Victoria will not be found to meet the requirements of a very much increased immigration, but will have to yield to the superior claims of Esquimalt, situated about three miles to the south-east. These places were connected by a road of the very worst description, a defect which I hope may, by this time, have been remedied. As far as I can remember, no great difficulties exist in the way of laying down a tramroad along this route. Esquimalt possesses a splendid harbour, consisting, properly speaking, of two harbours, each capable of receiving vessels of the largest tonnage, even to the "Great Eastern" herself. A whole fleet might here find secure anchorage. The town itself consists of little more than an assemblage of wooden huts, but is destined, eventually, I think, to become a place of importance. At the present moment, however, it owes its very existence to the facts of its being the chosen station of the men-of-war on this coast, as well as the port whence the mail steamer sails twice a month to San

Francisco. The arrival of this steamer creates no small stir and sensation in the colony, and great is the rush for letters at the Post Office in Victoria, as the very brief delay of the mail steamer at Esquimalt, seldom exceeding two or three hours, leaves but little time for answering correspondence. I cannot speak of the Postal arrangements of the colony without alluding to "Wells, Fargo, & Co., Express and Forwarding Agents." They are much in request for sending letters and parcels to San Francisco, as well as into the interior of British Columbia, as such missives, confided to their charge, are not only safer, but likely to reach their destination more speedily than by means of the ordinary mail conveyance.

On entering the inner harbour of which I have just spoken, the little town of Victoria may be discovered, scattered along its shore. At the time of my arrival in the colony, it consisted of little more than an assemblage of wooden houses; at the period of my departure, however, brick and stone were fast replacing the original wood, some handsome public buildings had been erected, and I observed several edifices of fireproof construction.

The first thing that strikes a European on approaching the shores of these distant regions, is the thoroughly wild and even savage character of the scenery; nor is this impression lessened as he discovers the huts of the aboriginal inhabitants, who, in their bizarre, party-coloured garments, may here and there be seen on the beach. Presently an angle in the bay reveals to him the burial-ground of these rude forefathers of the wilderness, with its quaint carvings and uncouth devices, the growth of a wild, untutored fancy, yet harmonizing strangely with the character of the surrounding scenery.

The country, in the vicinity of Victoria, is less densely wooded than in many other parts of the island, and oaks of stunted growth are met with in addition to the pine.

The general character of the district is hilly, and many open spaces exist perfectly sterile and covered with a débris of rocky fragments. There is, nevertheless, a considerable amount of agricultural and pastoral land, and numerous flourishing farms in the neighbourhood of the capital of Vancouver. Many extensive views, over the surrounding country and channel, may be enjoyed from the different heights about the town. Among these I would especially notice the varied and extensive prospect to be obtained from Cedar Hill. The view over the land embraces a vast extent of undulating, richly-wooded country, almost destitute, however, of any traces of human habitation; whilst over the sea, on a clear day, the eye embraces a vast extent of the blue surface of the channel, dotted with innumerable islands gradually losing themselves in the dim horizon. The entrance of the Gulf of

Georgia is a perfect archipelago, principal among the islands composing which we remark San Juan, the disputed claim to which so nearly involved us in a war with the United States.

## CHAPTER III.

Departure on our Cruise—A Night on the Island of San Juan—Depth of Water—Point Roberts—Fraser River—New Westminster, capital of British Columbia—Head-quarters of the Royal Engineers—" The Brunette "—Enormous Timber—Strong Current—Nanaimo—Coal on Vancouver's Island—A Hunting Expedition—Leave Nanaimo—Uculta Village—Valdez Island—Stiff Breeze—Dangerous Reef of Rocks—Fort Rupert.

THE yacht in which we performed our cruise round the Island of Vancouver, is a small vessel of twenty tons register, cutter rigged, which I took out with me on the deck of the ship in which we made our passage to Victoria. On my arrival in the colony I had her thoroughly fitted for sea. After various preparatory trial trips on the channel in the neighbourhood of Victoria, to test her sea-going qualities, we started in the month of September, 1860, on our cruise round the island, which we expected would take us about six weeks to accomplish, but we soon found that we had not made sufficient allowance for the difficulties we should encounter in our expedition. We got fairly under weigh one day about two o'clock in the afternoon, and with a fair wind and smooth sea made the Island of San Juan that night, and anchored off the camp of the Marines on the north coast of the island, in a small land-locked bay having all the appearance of an inland lake. Landing, in the evening, we were not sorry to warm ourselves at the fire at the back of the camp, and join the social circle of our friends the officers, assembled to enjoy their evening glass and pipe.

The island of San Juan, whose name was brought so prominently under the public notice some time since, in consequence of the unfounded claims put forth to its possession by the United States—claims so arrogantly backed by General Harney—is one of the group I have already specified, at the entrance to the Gulf of Georgia. Its strategic importance consists in its commanding two of the principal channels communicating with that gulf. That we were not involved in a war with the United States on this question I attribute mainly to the tact, judgment, and good sense displayed by Admiral, now Sir Lambert Baines, in his conduct of this delicate and irritating affair. The size of this island is about twelves miles in length, by seven or eight in width. Its general character is hilly, but not densely wooded.

The next morning saw us steering with a fair wind for the mouth of the Fraser River, but the wind was not sufficiently powerful to enable us to make way against the tide, which was running out with tremendous force. At length, after drifting for some hours, we found we were slowly advancing, a proof that the tide had turned; our progress was, however, very gradual, and our patience was sorely taxed ere we reached Saturna Island. Early on this day, finding that we had made no way against the current, we had recourse to our sweeps and pulled close in shore, hoping to find an anchorage; our first sounding gave ten fathoms, but immediately afterwards, on letting go the kedge, we failed to make it hold, though we paid out sixty fathoms. We anchored that night in comparatively shallow water, but found with all our efforts we could not get up our anchor next morning, so we cut our cable, and left a handspike attached to mark the spot.

The next day was calm, but night coming on with wind and rain we anchored off Point Roberts. The wind gradually increasing in violence, we felt no small anxiety lest our anchor should fail to hold. Towards morning the weather became less wild, and during the day we landed at Point Roberts, on the United States territory, near the mouth of the Fraser River. This place seems, originally, to have been destined for an extensive settlement.

There are some twenty or thirty houses standing, but not more than two or three are inhabited ; we were very pleased to receive a supply of fresh vegetables here, consisting of pumpkins, turnips, carrots, potatoes, and other equally acceptable esculents.

Entering the Fraser River next day, we signalled for a pilot to the Indian village near the mouth of the river. After a deal of gesticulating and waving flags, an old Indian was induced to put off in a canoe, with whom we struck a bargain to be taken up to New Westminster. We were compelled to wait some time for wind and tide to change, and then it was only after a long and tedious day's work that we at length found ourselves abreast New Westminster, capital of British Columbia.

The town of New Westminster stands on a rising ground on the left bank of the Fraser. The site it occupies—a clearing in the midst of a dense pine-forest—was selected by Colonel Moody, thus shifting the site originally fixed upon for the capital at Langley, a Hudson's Bay fort higher up the river. This was done for strategic reasons, as Langley is situated on the Southern or American bank of the river. Early in 1859 a communication was forwarded to the Colonial Secretary of State from Governor Douglas to the effect that her subjects in the colony were desirous that Her Majesty should name the metropolis they were about to found. The desire was at once graciously complied with, Her Majesty deciding that the capital of British Columbia should be called New Westminster. The growth of this town has been very rapid, and it is likely speedily to become a place of no small importance, in consequence of the recent discovery of gold. Up to the period of my departure from the colony, most of the houses were still of wood—nor had the Governor any official residence here.

New Westminster is well situated for commerce; the Fraser River is here some 2,000 yards wide, and vessels of considerable size can anchor off the town. About a mile higher up the river are the quarters of the Royal Engineers, situated on a steep incline, presenting a most picturesque *coup d'œil* from whichever side it is approached, both on account of the graceful, high-pitched roofs of the buildings themselves, as well as the romantic character of the site they occupy. The choice of this situation certainly reflects great credit, at least, on the taste of Colonel Moody, as, the river here forming an angle, a most extensive prospect may, in fine weather, be enjoyed—not only of its richly-wooded banks, but of the blue ranges of lofty mountains that shut in the distant horizon.

The Brunette, a most charming little river, forms a junction with the Fraser a short distance higher up. We frequently ascended this stream—a task, however, of no small difficulty, as its course is much impeded by fallen trees, some partially submerged, some forming a natural bridge across its narrower portions, and often so close to the surface of the water, that we had to stoop in our little boat to pass under them. We amused ourselves occasionally with shooting the bird here called grouse on its banks, and also succeeded in knocking over a partridge or two; but the dense nature of the undergrowth renders the pursuit of game a matter of no small personal injury and inconvenience, if not of absolute impossibility.

A little below New Westminster an extensive steam saw-mill has been established, which deals in a very summary way with the gigantic timber of these regions. I have already alluded to the size attained by the fir in this part of the world. My readers will, however, hardly be prepared to hear that a novice, having laid a wager to cut through a selected specimen with an axe, in three week's time, actually found himself, in spite of his most strenuous efforts, unable to accomplish his task. However incredible this may appear, it is an undoubted fact.

On descending the Fraser River we were again detained for a short time by a turn of tide, there being no wind whatever; we therefore availed ourselves of the opportunity to try and knock over a few wild-fowl among the swamps and shallows, which, at this time of year, afford shelter to innumerable flocks of ducks and geese. We were very successful; and, in addition to enjoying a good day's sport, managed to replenish our larder for some days to come. At length, the wind freshening, we were obliged to rejoin our little craft, and dropped down the stream. On reaching the mouth of the river at nightfall, we naturally anchored to await daylight, and, as we lay during the silent hours of the night with two anchors out, we could not fail to be struck with the tremendous force of the current, which, parting with a roaring sound under our bow, rushed along the sides of our little vessel with the impetuosity of a mill-stream. The uneasiness we naturally felt lest she should part from her anchors under this tremendous strain was not diminished by the very dense fog, which shrouded all objects in impenetrable darkness. We had hoped that morning might have dispelled the fog; instead of this being the case, however, it continued unabated all day, and we had to make up our minds to spend another night of anxiety and discomfort; for not only were we kept awake by the uneasy feeling that our cutter might drag her anchors, but the noise of the water under our bows was sufficiently great to render comfortable repose very difficult of attainment. The succeeding day being clear and fine, we were enabled to cross the bar, and once fairly at sea again, a fine breeze carried us across the Gulf of Georgia to Nanaimo. I may mention that Vancouver, to whom is due the honour of having first explored this channel, strangely enough overlooked the mouth of the Fraser River, although he did not fail to notice the discoloration of the waters of the Gulf of Georgia caused by its influx.

Nanaimo is a Hudson's Bay Fort, on the coast of Vancouver's Island. The small settlement which has recently sprung up bearing the same name, probably owes its existence entirely to the fact of its being a coaling station. It occupies the centre of the coaling district, that is to say, the only part of the Island of Vancouver in which coal is actually worked. This important mineral is, however, known to exist in various other portions of the colony. I am bound to confess that the so-called "Nanaimo coal" is not of the very finest description, although by no means despicable. It is used by the steamers of the Royal Navy, as well as by the vessels of the Pacific Steam Packet Company, and also finds a market in San Francisco; the line of steamers plying between the latter place and Panama prefer using the coal brought from Cardiff, of which a store exists at Acapulco, in Mexico.

During our stay at Nanaimo we organized a hunting expedition in the neighbourhood, with the view of providing ourselves with a little venison.

We set off one afternoon in a couple of small boats, a party of seven—six white men and an Indian, who enjoyed the reputation of being a crack shot. After a pull of some two hours we reached our destination on the shores of a bay, higher up the coast. Before landing we observed some lights on shore, it being at that time quite dark; these, we naturally conjectured, must belong to a party of Indians on their way from the North to Victoria, and we were for some time dubious whether it would be quite prudent to set foot on shore under the circumstances. Having, at length, overcome our scruples on this score, we discovered that the lights were those of a party of white men— American grasscutters and haymakers—who were collecting forage in a couple of canoes. After fraternizing we proceeded to bivouac, lit our fires, pitched our tents, and prepared our evening meal. While sitting round our camp-fire, before retiring to our couch for the night, we could not help observing the amount of labour bestowed by our Indian comrade on the weapon he carried, an old-fashioned flint-lock fowling-piece. He spent upwards of an hour cleaning most thoroughly its different parts, appearing especially solicitous that all in connection with the lock and pan for priming should be in first-rate order. It must be confessed, however, that the amount of sport enjoyed by any of our party next day by no means answered our expectations. The dense nature of the undergrowth of brushwood, and the huge masses of rock continually cropping out, rendered the pursuit of game, or indeed progression of any kind a matter of no small difficulty. As for myself, I only succeeded in knocking over a few birds. On returning to Nanaimo we had a regular battle against wind and tide, with the unpleasant accompaniment of driving rain. I may mention that on the shores of the bay where we encamped, we observed the remains of an Indian village, said to have belonged to a tribe now extinct, probably exterminated by continued warfare.

On leaving Nanaimo a few days after in company with the schooner "Langley," a small coasting trader, we found the navigation of the Gulf of Georgia very ticklish work, from the number of sunken rocks, on which we, more than once, were within an inch of stranding our little craft. After anchoring for the night, the first appearance of day revealed to us the dangers of our situation; we had selected a spot surrounded by sunken rocks, and we also found that what we had taken for a creek was, in reality, a passage between two islands not marked in the chart. Five canoes of Stickeen Indians came alongside, they told us a long story of the treachery of the Ucultas, which will be found in another part of our narrative. We started next morning with a nice breeze, and soon left the

"Langley" behind. The wind was afterwards for some time shifting and variable; at length, about ten, it was round to the right quarter once more, and we found ourselves within a mile of Cape Mudge, the most southerly point of Valdez Island.

Before we had time to congratulate ourselves on our progress, we were suddenly involved in a tide-rip, which, in a very short time, carried us back some six or seven miles. We were now abreast of the "Langley" again, but she fared no better than we did, and after drifting about until the tide became slack, we pulled into soundings, and let go our anchors. The Uculta village is situated on Johnson's Straits; they are reputed the worst Indians anywhere to be met with about here, plundering and killing those of the northern tribes, whenever they met with them. We did not find the current as strong as we anticipated next morning. We made fast, when the tide failed us, in a little bay, or bight, of Valdez Island; and going on shore to look for a deer, saw the traces not only of many of these animals, but also of wolf and bear. We only succeeded, however, in wounding one deer. Landing on Vancouver next day we were equally unsuccessful, as we did not discover anything to shoot. We anchored for the night off an island at the entrance of Knox Bay, and started next morning with a fair breeze, which had a tendency to freshen as the day advanced. The tide with us till about eleven, running strong, and forming in places violent eddies—the sea was also much encumbered with floating timber, which rendered navigation difficult and dangerous, as many of the trunks were of gigantic size. The wind blew very fresh, after a temporary lull, and put us down so much by the bows that we took in our gaff-topsail, and she went more easily in consequence. The tide ran for some four hours against us, but the breeze was sufficiently powerful to enable us to hold on our course, as it was now blowing half a gale of wind. We had some difficulty in clearing the rocks in front of the Nimkish village—our vessel jibed, breaking her guy, and carrying away some of her running-tackle, but doing little other damage. Almost before we had time, however, to ascertain what injury we had sustained, we had left the rocks, the cause of our late anxiety, far behind. We reached Fort Rupert about six in the evening, followed in about an hour afterwards by the " Langley," thoroughly satisfied with our day's run, having done some 90 miles in eleven hours.

## CHAPTER IV.

Indian Tribes inhabiting Vancouver's Island—Northern Indians visiting the Island periodically—Enmity among the Different Tribes—Indian Warfare—Weapons—Canoes—Treachery of the Ucultas—General Appearance of the Indians—Artificial Flattening of the Skull—Use of Paint—Indian Women—Dress—Indian Village—Huts—Fishing Season—Salmon—Articles of Food—Whisky—Carving—Construction of Canoe—Indian Burial-Ground—Mysteries of the Kluquolla—Gambling—Indian Superstitions.

So much has been written on the manners, customs, and natural traits of the aboriginal inhabitants of the great Continent of the West, that it might at first sight appear superfluous on my part to devote any considerable portion of my space to their consideration; but I am convinced that the general characteristics of this, as of all other races, are materially modified by the local circumstances of climate, soil, and the geographical features of the country they inhabit. The Indian tribes inhabiting the islands and seaboard of the Pacific differ in many essential particulars from those of the interior of the continent, and I consider that many of their habits and customs are sufficiently marked and interesting to merit a special notice; much of this information will, moreover, be found valuable to the intending emigrant and settler in these colonies.

It must always be a matter of no small difficulty to fix the number of Indians of different tribes who dwell permanently in the two colonies of British Columbia and Vancouver, nor can I regard any such estimate, at present, as being anything more than an approximative guess. In addition to the tribes here located, great numbers visit these regions during the summer months, often coming from a great distance to the north, and performing voyages by sea of many hundred miles in their canoes. Among the more numerous and powerful of these tribes I would mention the Hydahs, the Chimseeans, the Stickeens, the Skidegates, and the Bella-Bellas. They visit these shores for the purpose of disposing of the produce of their hunting expeditions, and return to their home in the far north at the approach of autumn, carrying with them the proceeds of their trading in the shape of money, blankets, powder, tobacco, whisky and other articles in use among them. I have, as a rule, remarked that the physical attributes of those tribes coming from the north are superior to those of the dwellers in the south.

Here, as elsewhere, we shall find the greatest enmity frequently existing among different tribes, some of them being constantly at war with one another. The origin of these quarrels, in many cases, dates from a very remote period; they are in fact hereditary feuds handed down from generation to generation. The deadly hate existing between hostile tribes is something almost incredible. Until quite recently members of different tribes, at war with one another, would forthwith proceed to extremities on meeting, even in the streets of Victoria itself, and at the present moment the utmost efforts of the authorities are ineffectual to prevent the frequent occurrence of murders in the vicinity of the town. The Chicklezats and the Ahazats, inhabiting districts in close proximity on the west coast of Vancouver, are accustomed to wage so unrelenting a warfare that no single member of either tribe can ever be induced for one moment to set foot on the territory of his hereditary enemy, too well knowing that he could only do so at the peril of his life. Treachery and artifice constitute the base of their tactics in war. They appear insensible to anything like chivalry or generous feeling, killing and slaying with remorseless cruelty, undeterred by any sentiment of compunction. Their motto appears to be, "All is fair in war." An assault may be expected at any moment from a hostile tribe during a period of open warfare, midnight attacks taking precedence of all others, and humanity shudders in recording the atrocities practised on such occasions. Previous to encountering the hardships and dangers of a campaign, if we may so term it, the Indian goes through a course of athletic training. He is rigidly abstemious, and among the methods employed to give tone to his muscles and strengthen his physical constitution I may notice the practice of constant bathing, even during very severe weather. The weapon most in vogue with these savage warriors is the long, smooth-bore, flint-lock musket, in addition to which they generally carry a long knife, having now to a great extent discarded the use of the traditional tomahawk and spear. Many of these weapons are, however, still preserved as heirlooms among them. Their general mode of fighting on shore is from the ambush of the trunks of trees, seldom exposing themselves to fire in the open. Engagements on the sea in their canoes are by no means of frequent occurrence. All prisoners taken in war are, if not slaughtered on the spot, doomed to perpetual slavery. As an instance of the dastardly treachery so frequently practised by one tribe towards another, I may mention the affair of the Ucultas and Stickeen Indians, to which I before alluded, and which was related to us by a party of the latter a few hours after it occurred. The former tribe, one of the most powerful located in Vancouver, are a band of lawless pirates and robbers, levying black-mail on all the surrounding tribes, and are held in universal dread and abhorrence. On the occasion referred to the Stickeen Indians, being on their journey from the North to Victoria in their canoes, put into a bight on the coast to await nightfall, intending to drop down silently with the tide, under cover of the darkness, so as to pass the village of their hereditary foes, the Ucultas, without their knowledge. One of the Uculta canoes happening to meet a couple of the Stickeen canoes engaged in fishing, the occupants of the former persuaded those of the latter that they had been so far won over by the teaching of the Roman Catholic missionaries as to have entirely abandoned their old malpractices, and that perfect confidence might therefore be placed in them, inviting the Stickeens at the same time to land and share their hospitality on shore. The latter, though far from convinced, thought it prudent not to show any symptoms of fear, as the fact of their being in the neighbourhood would now be well known. The whole party of the Stickeens, therefore, accompanied the Ucultas to their village. Laying down their arms at the request of the latter, who, while professing nothing but friendship and goodwill, were not disposed to place implicit confidence in the

Stickeens, they accompanied their hosts on shore, leaving the canoes in the charge of their women and children. They paid, however, dearly for their confidence, as they were betrayed into an ambush and several of them killed on the spot, the remnant only escaping with their lives by precipitate flight, two of them being badly wounded, whom we afterwards saw lying at the bottom of a canoe.

The general physical characteristics of these races do not differ very essentially from those of the interior of the mainland. We meet with the same high cheek-bones, broad flat faces, thick but not prominent lips, strait black hair, sallow complexions verging towards copper colour, and spare muscular forms, with which former descriptions have already made us familiar. The eyes and hair are universally dark, and the latter being worn long, its thick, unkempt masses frequently form the only covering for the head. An Indian never cuts his hair, as short hair is a mark of slavery. Any difference is chiefly one of degree, and, as I before remarked, some of the finest specimens I saw came from the far north. I am bound to confess, however, that much of the romance with which I had in youth been led to invest the wild denizen of the vast unexplored regions of the west, from a perusal of Fenimore Cooper's novels, and others of a similar class, was dispelled by a personal acquaintance. Many of the tribes inhabiting Vancouver and the adjacent coasts, practise the barbarous custom of flattening the skull by means of two pieces of wood bound tightly to the fore part of the head, in infancy and childhood, whereby the skull is forced into an unnatural and hideous shape, rising, in fact, to a perfect ridge on the top. Some tribes distort their skulls into a shape that has been likened to a sugar-loaf. As far as I could ascertain, this strange interference with the normal development of the brain is not attended by any mental deficiency. Most tribes are accustomed to pierce the ears and nose, in which rings of moderate size are worn; to those in the ear, however, many other pendants are generally attached. I have frequently been amused to see an Indian, on receiving the always welcome gift of two or three English needles, carry them away with him stuck in the hole pierced through his nostril. The most unsightly of these customs is that of piercing the lower lip. This is confined entirely to the Northern Indians, and among them is only practised by the women. In the earlier stages, a small silver tube is worn through the puncture; with the lapse of years, however, the size of this article is gradually increased, until at length the lip comes to be distended to a hideous extent by the insertion of a shell or wooden ornament. Tattooing is also occasionally seen among some of the tribes coming from the north. The custom of occasionally painting the face is universal, and the pigments in use for this purpose constitute an important article of barter in Indian trading. Vermilion is in special demand, great quantities of this colour being used during the period of the mysteries or initiation of the Kluquolla, as it is termed, to which I shall refer hereafter. Their black or war paint, they manufacture themselves. This colour is an invariable indication of war; at the same time its use is not confined to the battle-field, as it is also a sign of mourning, and is frequently employed by the fair sex to preserve their delicate complexions from the too ardent rays of the sun! Having mentioned the ladies, I am bound to acknowledge that I have sometimes seen faces which might be described as pleasing, as well as not ungraceful figures, among the younger women, but a due regard for truth obliges me to add that their charms, if any be discoverable, are very short-lived. One of the chief defects in both sexes is their very awkward walk, or rather waddle, caused by their legs and feet being cramped and deformed, and their toes turned in, from constantly sitting in their canoes.

The dress in use among many of the more remote tribes, may be described as a simple blanket, with the addition of a garment of their own manufacture, consisting of strips of bark, fastened round the waist, and worn by the women. Others, more advanced in civilization, indulge in the use of shirts, in addition to their blankets. An Indian village consists of an assemblage of huts, arranged in a line. It may not, however, be generally known to my readers that an Indian village is, to a certain extent, a mere temporary encampment. Every tribe has two or three villages, in various situations—their locality being determined by the facilities it may afford for pursuing the avocations of hunting and fishing, at different periods of the year. An Indian hut consists of a framework of posts and beams, often of gigantic proportions, as in the case of a chief or head of a tribe. This frame is always left standing, but the outer planking is removed every time the tribe shifts its quarters. Of course it is needless to add that all their household goods and chattels travel with them, on every occasion. The cutting out the huge planks, with which the huts are covered and roofed, with the imperfect tools and appliances at the command of the Indians, is a work at least of great labour and perseverance. Indians are skilful huntsmen, and many of them are very good shots. They are not very particular as to the kind of game wherewith to stock their larder—the flesh of very few animals comes amiss to an Indian palate. The fishing season is an important period for those inhabiting the coast. Their sea-fish are always taken with a hook, the original article of native manufacture being almost superseded by English fish-hooks. They are very skilful fishermen, and I have often admired the noiseless manner in which they steer their canoes through the water, when trolling for salmon. This fine fish is everywhere met with throughout the waters of Vancouver, and frequently attains a large growth. Those of the Fraser River are distinguished by the peculiarity of their nose being twisted on one side, which gives them a very comical appearance. I do not know whether this phenomenon can be accounted for by the force of the current these fish have to stem. In addition to this deformity, the bodies of the salmon taken out of this river, are frequently much scored, gashed, and disfigured by old wounds, the result of accident, and arising from collision with the rocks and shallows of this impetuous stream. Sturgeon of gigantic size, weighing at times as much as five or six hundred pounds, are also taken in the Fraser River. There are various Indian modes of curing salmon, the ordinary one being to split them open, and hang them up to dry, distended with pegs, in the smoky atmosphere of their huts. This gives them much the appearance of kippered salmon, to which, however, they are very inferior in flavour. In their migrations from one village to another, the Indians frequently leave a stock of this salmon behind them, packed in boxes, and deposited at some height among the branches of the trees, for their use on a future occasion. The true Indian method of cooking a salmon consists in putting it into a wooden bowl with water, which is made to boil by dropping in red-hot stones. The only vegetable we have ever seen in use among the Indians, is the potatoe, which is readily purchased by those tribes that are acquainted with it. Many imported articles of food in use among the colonists are rapidly being adopted by them, such as flour, biscuits, rice, sugar, and molasses, the latter being a special favourite. Spirits of the vilest description are supplied them by the whisky-sellers, a proscribed class, as a very severe penalty justly attaches to selling any kind of ardent spirits, the very bane and curse of his race, to an Indian. Yet, so great is the passionate longing of the red man for the fatal fire-water, that he will run all risks, and part with his most valued possessions to obtain it, and, to the disgrace of civilization be it recorded, that white men can be found sufficiently vile and degraded to pander to the weakness of the poor savage, by supplying him with an intoxicating alcoholic compound of the most worthless and unwholesome description.

The custom of executing quaint carvings in wood, bone, and other substances for which the Indians have long been noted, seems falling into disuse. The specimens now produced are nothing like so

E

curious and elaborate as the older ones. The Indian canoe has been celebrated ever since the white man was first brought into contact with the aboriginal inhabitants of America. The well-known bark canoe met with among the Indian races of the interior I have never seen here. The canoe of this part of the world is fashioned out of the trunk of a single tree; they are of various sizes, and, I need hardly assure my readers that, even with the improved implements obtainable by the Indians in the present day, they are a work of no small labour. They are hollowed out by a slow fire, so disposed under the trunk to be operated upon as to consume the inner portion. In the war canoe the prow is elevated, being intended to afford shelter to its occupants; the top part is also furnished with a groove on which to rest their musket in firing. Rudely fashioned as they may appear, in the hands of an Indian crew these vessels are wonderfully buoyant and sea-worthy; at the same time, the Indian is by no means fond of exposing himself to bad weather at sea, and will wait for days before putting out, if it appears likely to blow. The paddles are, generally speaking, made of deal, and differ but slightly in form among the various tribes, some few of them are cut to a point. Friendly tribes will sometimes challenge each other to trials of speed in their canoes. It is a common practice of the Indians to bury their dead in a canoe, which is dragged on shore for the purpose, the body being enveloped in a blanket and laid therein, surrounded by the weapons and other articles used by the deceased in his lifetime, and thus, that which was almost his home in life becomes his sepulchre in death. The burial-grounds are generally situated at some distance from the village, and present a rude assemblage of the boxes and canoes which form the last resting-places of their dead. The Indians never inter their dead. An island is very frequently selected as a place of burial, and I remember landing on one containing an immense number of Indian tombs, in fact quite a cemetery, if I may so term it, and which we named "Deadman's Island" in consequence. Among some tribes the custom is prevalent of placing their dead in boxes among the branches of trees. I have been informed that incremation is practised by some tribes, but I never met with an instance of it myself.

Among the most singular of Indian customs, must certainly be enumerated the ceremonies attending the initiation of a candidate into the mysteries of the "Kluquolla," as it is termed, which seems to constitute a species of freemasonry, and is practised by all the tribes I ever came into contact with. The aspirant to this privilege and honour has to submit to a very severe preparatory ordeal. He is removed from his own dwelling by a party of those who are already Kluquollas, and led to a hut set apart for his special use. The first ceremony consists in cutting the arteries under the tongue, and allowing the blood to flow over his body, the face being, meanwhile, covered with a mask. After this an opiate is administered, which induces a state of unconsciousness, in which he is allowed to remain two days. At the end of this time he is plunged, or rather thrown headlong into the water to arouse him. As soon as he is fully awaked, he rushes on shore, and, as a rule, seizes the first dog he perceives with his teeth, tears, lacerates, and even devours a portion of it, at least so I have been credibly informed. I can only speak from personal observation as to some portions of the singular ceremonies in practice on these occasions, as the Indians are very jealous of any interference on the part of a white man. He also bites any of his fellows whom he may meet with. It is said that they who are already Kluquollas esteem it rather an honour to be thus bitten. He is now seized, bound with ropes, and led like a captive, by the party in charge of him, three times a day round the village during a period of seven days, a rattle producing a dreadful noise being constantly agitated before him. At this time he bites and stabs indiscriminately every one he comes across, and as he certainly would not spare a white man if he happened to meet him in the camp, I took good care to keep both my own person and that of a favourite little dog out of his reach. At night he is bound to a tree, and is supposed during the whole of this period to eat nothing whatever. I shrewdly suspect, however, that he is provided with food by the women during the night. At the end of the eighth day, being in a thoroughly weak and exhausted state, food and stimulants are administered, and he is gradually restored to his normal condition, when he affects great contrition for his former excesses, and after passing a couple of days in a state of tearful repentance, he is from that time forward a free and accepted Kluquolla.

Among the vices of the Indians I must not forget to enumerate, in addition to drunkenness, a passion for gambling. An Indian, when excited by play, will stake everything he possesses, to the blanket on his shoulders. A game is played among themselves, with a number of small pieces of polished stick, about five inches in length, and having much the appearance of short pencils. These are enveloped from time to time, by the players on either side, in a mass of bark fibre or tow, and then dealt out like a pack of cards with great rapidity. I do not profess to offer any explanation of the nature of the game in question, as I never could arrive at anything like a satisfactory comprehension of it. That it possesses great attractions for the Indians themselves, however, is evidenced by the fact that they will sit for hours together engaged in it.

Of the religious belief of the Indians, it is very difficult to speak with anything like confidence. I have often taken considerable pains to question them on this subject, but could never elicit any satisfactory exposition of their particular creed; whatever this may be, it is of course mixed up with fables and superstitions of the grossest kind. For the subjoined list of Indian traditions, I am indebted to a number of the *Victoria Daily British Colonist*. I give them, with certain modifications and alterations of my own, for what they are worth, without pledging myself to the authority of any one of them, except that relating to the deluge, to which I have myself heard Indians refer.

The belief among the Northern Indians is, first, that Yale (crow) made everything. That men possess a never-dying soul. The brave, who fall in battle, and those who are murdered, enjoy everlasting happiness in heaven; while those that die a natural death are condemned to dwell for ages among the branches of tall trees. The world was originally dark, shapeless, chaotic, the only living thing being Yale. For a long time he flew round and round the watery waste, until at length, growing weary of the intolerable solitude, he determined to people the universe. He bade the waters recede, and the sun shine forth and dry the earth. The effect of this was to cause a dense mist to arise; out of this mist he created salmon, and put them into the lakes and rivers. Birds and beasts were afterwards created on land. After Yale had finished his work of creation he made a survey of it, and found that all creatures were satisfied with the universe in which they had been placed, with the exception of the lizard, who, having a stock of provisions laid up for winter use, and being moreover a great sleeper, preferred a request to be allowed five months' winter. "Not so," replied Yale, "for the sake of the other animals there shall be but four snowy months." The lizard insisted on five, stretching forth at the same time his five digits, for in those days he had a hand like a man. The crow seized his hand, and cutting off one finger gave him to understand that the remaining number should indicate the months of the seasons, four rainy, four snowy, and four summer. The crow finding, as winter came on, that he had no house to shelter him, or to store the salmon he had prepared for winter use, made two men to build houses. He then taught them how to make ropes out of the bark of trees, and to dry salmon. After a time, feeling the want of a helpmate, the crow began to look out for a wife. His first choice fell upon a salmon, but, having treated his first spouse so badly that she left him, he began to look out for a second, and this time married a young lady belonging to the sun, who bore him a son, which youth, evidently the Phæton of the Indian mythology, attempting to guide the course of the sun, the latter grew unmanageable, and came so near the earth as to parch and burn up everything. The old crow, however, came to his assistance, and restored the luminary of day to its proper orbit. One day Yale went to Nass River and asked the people for something to eat. They replied they were too poor to offer him anything; he therefore created salmon for them and put it into their river. Another time the all-important crow made a morning call on an old acquaintance named Cannook. Being tired and thirsty towards nightfall, he asked for a bed and something to drink. Cannook told him he might lodge under his roof, but water, he for some incomprehensible reasons of his own, positively refused to supply him with. When all had retired to rest, the crow seized the opportunity of assuaging his thirst, but Cannook's wife perceiving him, called out to her husband, who jumped up and threw some wood on the fire. The crow tried to escape by the hole in the roof for letting out the smoke, but Cannook kept piling on fresh wood, and the result was that, before the crow could extricate himself, he was as thoroughly black and smoke-dried as a London sparrow. From the period of this notable adventure the great crow and all his descendants, from having been white before, became perfectly black. A long time after the creation of all things by Yale, a serious misunderstanding arose between the crow and the inhabitants of the world he had made. To punish them he therefore sent a deluge. The clouds grew dark and lowering, rain fell in torrents, the rocks opened and poured forth streams of water. At length the waters rose until the face of the earth was hidden, and all people took refuge in their canoes. Higher still rose the flood, until all but the summits of three very lofty mountains were covered. To these numbers, who had no canoes, fled; many of the latter were upset, and their occupants drowned. Finally, the waters began to subside, and the earth was once more dry and habitable.

The missionaries of the Romish Church have long laboured assiduously among these different Indian tribes, and with considerable apparent success in some instances, especially among the Cowichins, a good many of whom attend mass in the little chapel of the mission. There is now a very effective staff of Protestant missionaries in Vancouver, equally zealous in the task of conversion. A school, exclusively for Indians, has been established at Victoria on the Indian reserve, which is attended by both children and adults, who receive secular and religious instruction. They were beginning to learn the use of written characters when I left, and I have heard a chapter in the Bible translated and expounded to them in Chinnook, as well as the

Decalogue with the very appropriate introduction of an eleventh commandment—'Wake klosh muck-a-muck whisky: " "Thou shalt not drink whisky;" or as it stands in Chinnook, "It is not good to drink whisky." Much of the success of this institution is due to the tact and energy of the master, a clergyman of the Church of England, who, to his other undoubted qualifications for the post he fills, is adding a knowledge of several Indian dialects.

## CHAPTER V.

Indian Servants—Mode of Dealing with Indians—Misconduct of the Hydahs—They Fire on the "Rob Roy"—Prompt Measures taken by the Authorities to Redress the Outrage—The Hydahs are brought to reason—Captain John—His Capture and Death—Adventure of the Cowichin Indian—Northern Marauders—Lieutenant Robson sets out in Pursuit—Insolent Defiance of the Indians—Effect of the Great Guns—The Ucultas—Fort Rupert—Excellent Garden—Kindness of the Chief Factor—We leave Fort Rupert—Round the North-west Point of the Island—Carried by the Tide past our Destination—Quatsinough Harbour—Koshkeemo Village—Our Indian Host—The Interior of a Hut—Domestic Life—Indian Apathy.

My long sojourn among the Indians of different tribes inhabiting the coasts of Vancouver's Island, did not tend to impress me with a high opinion of the morality of the untutored savage. I regard them as being, generally speaking, treacherous and deceitful, and cannot help looking on every Indian as more or less a thief at heart. In common with all their race, they possess the savage attributes of a wonderfully passive endurance of hardship and suffering, and a stoic indifference to torture and death when inevitable, which amounts to a kind of rude heroism. Of their natural courage there can be no doubt. If they can be preserved from the curse of drinking, they are frugal and abstemious in their way of living, and, although not fond of work, they can be taught to acquit themselves creditably of any ordinary task that may be assigned them, and make in many cases very fair household servants. At the same time, an Indian does not willingly take service among the white men, or, at least, only does so with a view of amassing sufficient money to buy blankets and other coveted articles wherewith to astonish his kinsfolk, and increase his own dignity when he returns to his native woods. To this period of emancipation he looks constantly forward during the whole time of his service, and, however settled and domesticated he may appear, he is sure to startle his employers some fine morning with the announcement that he is about to return to savage life. At the same time, whatever may be my opinion of the Indian himself, I would strongly impress on all colonists to observe strict veracity and perfect good faith in all their dealings with Indians, who are accustomed to look upon the word of a white man as a bond. The credit of the entire community would therefore be imperilled by anything like dishonest practices. As a proof of the implicit confidence placed by Indians inhabiting the more remote districts, in the white man, we may mention that they are always willing to accept his promise in writing to pay for any commodities they may have furnished him with.

By way of giving my readers a few practical illustrations of the different traits and characteristics of Indian life and manners, I subjoin the following anecdotes, for the veracity of which I can vouch. The Hydah Indians, whose camp was in the neighbourhood of Victoria, had for some time been very troublesome to the authorities. Becoming gradually bolder and more insolent, they at length brought matters to a climax by firing on the "Rob Roy," a small trading schooner, as she was leaving the Harbour of Victoria. A boat was forthwith sent back, and Mr. Pemberton, Chief of Police, was informed of the outrage committed. A body of policemen were soon in readiness, and were at once despatched to the Hydah camp, to demand of the chiefs that the offenders should be given up to justice, and that the entire tribe should surrender their arms. This was peremptorily and even insolently refused; the Hydahs seeming to be possessed with the idea that they were sufficiently numerous and powerful to measure strength with the white men. After a second ineffectual application, the Governor, acting in concert with the Admiral of the Fleet, took such measures as he thought would be effectual in reducing the Hydahs to reason, without unnecessary bloodshed. A couple of launches, with their crews, were despatched from Esquimalt to make a demonstration in front, while a body of marines was sent overland to take up a position in the rear of the Indian encampment. On the appearance of the launches a final application was made, giving the Hydahs ten minutes to consider their answer. They held out doggedly until a bugle call summoned forth the marines from their ambush in the rear of the camp. At the sight of the redjackets they at once changed their tone, and the delinquents were given up barely a moment before the time specified; all arms in the camp were at the same time secured, with the understanding, however, that they were to be given up again to the Indians on their quitting the colony. The offenders were taken to Victoria, tried, and then publicly flogged in the midst of the Hydah camp, a great disgrace in the eyes of an Indian. A few days afterwards another misunderstanding arose between this tribe and the police, the exact origin of which we forget; it ended, however, in the arrest of two of the Hydah chiefs, the so-called Captain John, whom we had known well in Victoria, and his brother. As soon as they reached their destination—the police station in Victoria—and it was attempted to incarcerate them, they showed fight, and Captain John giving a signal to his brother, both produced their knives, and made a desperate onslaught on the police. Quick as were the Hydahs in producing their knives, the police were equally ready with their revolvers, and, at the second or third shot, Captain John fell mortally wounded. The report of this event spread rapidly among the Hydahs, and it was soon known far to the northward that an Indian had been killed by the white men at Victoria. The very rapid manner in which news of any kind travels through the island would almost lead to the belief that the Indians had established something like a chain of posts for the conveyance of intelligence. The real fact of the matter is that news is conveyed along the coast from the crew of one canoe to another, as they meet on their different fishing grounds; and on the occasion of our first visit to Nanaimo we received a strong hint from some friendly Indians, that it would be prudent for us to leave on account of the number of Hydahs in the neighbourhood of that station, who might be disposed to avenge the death of their kinsman on the white population generally.

As a proof of the coolness and courage an Indian is capable of displaying, as well as of the unswerving constancy with which he adheres to the realization of a design once conceived, I may relate the following trait as I received it from the master of the principal actor in the adventure I record. A boy of the Cowichin tribe, inhabiting the vicinity of Victoria, was captured by a party of Hydahs going north. They took him with them to their home, distant some seven or eight hundred miles from the place of his birth. The Cowichin youth, from the very first moment of his capture, conceived the design of escaping whenever an opportunity should occur, which did not however present itself for years, as he was most jealously guarded by his captors. He was, of course, condemned to perpetual slavery, but was not apparently badly treated in other respects. At length, after having been detained some twelve or fourteen years, as far as I could understand from his account, the rigour of the surveillance to which he was subjected having been to some extent relaxed, the long-desired, long watched-for opportunity did at length occur, and he made his escape in a small canoe, taking with him a few fishing-lines to provide himself with food on his long and perilous journey. Thus, unbefriended and alone, without chart or compass, did this poor savage paddle forth in his frail bark on a voyage of many hundred miles, over the rolling waves of the mighty Pacific. After encountering innumerable dangers and hardships, and after many hairbreadth escapes from death or captivity among hostile tribes, he at length reached his destination, and rejoined his kindred in Vancouver's Island.

During the period of my stay in the colony, a couple of white men arrived in a canoe at Victoria, bringing with them the intelligence that a party of Northern Indians, on their way home, had landed, broken into their house, and after plundering it of almost everything, proceeded on their journey. This occurred at Salt Spring Island, some fifty or sixty miles from Victoria. An order was at once issued to get the gunboat "Forward" ready for sea, and to put forth in pursuit of the Indians—an order which its gallant commander, the late Lieutenant Robson, was not long in carrying into execution. After calling at Nanaimo for an interpreter, they came upon the Indians, encamped at Cape Mudge, Valdez Island. A message was forthwith sent on shore, summoning the chiefs to deliver up the offenders. This was insolently refused, the Indians adding that they cared nothing about the little "no-good schooner," as they contemptuously termed the gunboat, declaring that they could take her if they pleased, and even attempting to stop the boat that brought the message on shore from putting off. Having had no experience of the power of artillery, they affected to treat the "great guns" with disdain, thinking that it was merely intended to overawe them by their size, and that they were in reality made rather for show than use. They were, however, soon undeceived by Lieutenant Robson, who opened fire on some empty canoes, which were speedily smashed to atoms. The Indians now retreated to the woods, and shots were exchanged on both sides. The rifle-plates having been set up on board the gunboat to protect his men, Lieutenant Robson sent a few charges of grape flying and crashing through the branches of the trees over the heads of the Indians, with the humane view of sparing unnecessary slaughter. While this was going on, the neighbouring tribe of the Ucultas gathered in their canoes like a swarm of bees round the gunboat, perfectly delighted at the turn matters had taken, and offering their services to the white men, in the event of an assault being made on shore, eager to seize the opportunity of avenging themselves, with the aid of such powerful allies, on their hereditary enemies, the Northern Indians, an offer which I need not say was refused. The latter being now convinced that they had to deal with a much more formidable foe than they had anticipated, a party of them made their appearance on the beach, displaying a white flag of truce. A parley ensued, which ended in the surrender of the chiefs, who were taken to Victoria for trial and punishment. Lieutenant Robson insisting that all arms should be delivered up, the order was complied with; but on representation having been made to him that by so doing these unhappy Indians would be placed entirely at the mercy of the Ucultas, of whose deadly hatred towards them the white men had received a proof during the fight, he consented to restore them. From that day forth the highest possible respect was felt for the "great guns" by all the Indian tribes inhabiting the surrounding districts.

Fort Rupert, called after the princely founder of the Hudson's Bay Company, is situated on the north-east coast of Vancouver's Island, and presents the usual characteristics of this class of building, which I will briefly describe for the benefit of those who have never seen one of these forts. It consists of a quadrangle enclosed by a lofty stockade, made of the tall pine-trees felled in the immediate vicinity, sunk some considerable distance into the ground, and kept together by cross-beams on the inside. There is a gallery running round the interior of this enclosure, which just allows a man to walk upright protected from an enemy's fire. At two opposite corners of the quadrangle are flanking bastions, mounting, in the case of Fort Rupert, four 9-pounders each, sweeping the sides of the fort and the adjacent country. Some of these forts, however, mount heavier guns. The garden and outbuildings are protected by smaller stockades. Inside the fort itself are various houses for drying and storing furs, for trading with the

Indians, for stores, for workshops, labourers' cottages, and other purposes, together with the residence of the chief officer in command.

Fort Rupert is situated on a natural harbour of a very imperfect kind. Such insecure anchorage does it afford that, in consequence of the high wind, which continued during the whole night after our arrival, no one on board the cutter got a wink of sleep, but she fortunately held to her anchors gallantly. The fort itself is situated in the centre of the village of the Cogwell Indians, having, of course, a clear sea frontage. The country round it has been partially cleared of timber, as a considerable quantity has been cut for the use of the "Beaver," the "Otter," and the "Labouchere" steamers engaged in the Hudson's Bay trade. I believe that steam navigation was introduced into the North Pacific by the Hudson's Bay Company,—their steamer, the "Old Beaver" as she is termed, being the first ever seen on these coasts. We were much struck with the high state of cultivation, as well as the extreme neatness of the garden of the fort. I had seen nothing to equal it since we left England, and may even go so far as to say that I have seldom seen a gentleman's garden in the old country better kept. We were received on landing by "Willie Mitchell," as he is familiarly termed throughout the colony—the chief trader in command of the fort—to whom I was favoured with a letter of introduction, and from whom we received every kindness during our stay. We thoroughly inspected the fort, with its rooms for drying and storing furs, its different workshops, forges, labourers' cottages, and other buildings—a Hudson's Bay fort being a perfect little community in itself. The house of the chief trader in command was really a comfortable and spacious residence, containing some ten or twelve rooms, with the additional advantage of having no taxes to pay. After a couple of days' sojourn here, we again set sail, taking with us a supply of fresh vegetables and a fine buck, for which we were indebted to the kindness of the commander of the fort. Many of the turnips and carrots out of the garden were among the finest we had ever seen anywhere. It was a case of at once welcoming the coming and speeding the parting guest, as, well knowing, from long experience, the dangers of the navigation of the Pacific during the winter months, our friend Willie Mitchell urged upon us to lose no time in prosecuting our cruise, it being now the 16th of October, so as not to be on the outer coast of the island after the first week in November. We anchored on the first night after leaving Fort Rupert in Chucartie Harbour, on the extreme north of Vancouver's Island. Between this place and Cape Scott, where we anchored on the ensuing night, we were involved in a series of tide-rips, the currents being very strong off this coast. The night was clear and calm, with a heavy dew. Starting the next morning, we fully expected, after a run of an hour or two, to make Sea-Otter Harbour.

Our pilot was thoroughly unacquainted with this part of the coast, never having been here before; the consequence was that, although all on board kept a sharp look-out, we managed to pass the entrance to the bay. The rocky islets extend out from Cape Scott for a great distance to sea, and we sought in vain for any of Captain Richards's surveying marks along this portion of the coast.

By the time we were fully convinced that we must have passed our destination, we caught sight of a canoe, to which we signalled. After considerable hesitation and delay, the Indians, being evidently astonished and alarmed at our unwonted appearance, came alongside. As these Indians could not talk Chinnook, the ordinary medium of communication with all the tribes on the opposite coasts of the island, we were a long time before we could understand them. At length we made out that they were Quatsinoughs, and that their village lay beyond a point of land which we had determined to explore. We were somewhat startled by this announcement on the part of the Indians, as it made us some 24 miles further to the southward than we had intended to go that day, which would seem to prove that we had been carried along by a powerful current from the north. We pulled round the point indicated by the Indians, and came to an anchorage under the lee of a small island at the entrance of Quatsinough and Koshkeemo Harbour. There was a good deal of swell on during the night, and we had to let go a second anchor. In the early morning the same canoe we had seen the day before again came alongside, informing us of the exact locality of their village, some five or six miles higher up Quatsinough Harbour—they also pointed out a good anchorage.

Preparing to get under weigh, our smaller anchor defied our utmost efforts to raise it, and in the end our vessel, with the assistance of the rising tide and swell, succeeded in freeing it herself. We then gave her her sails and ran up Quatsinough Harbour; passing the spot where the "Eagle" was wrecked, some years before, in a gale of wind, we anchored in a snug little bight. We were soon surrounded by the canoes of the Quatsinoughs, and made several purchases from them of geese, rock-cod and other necessaries—paying them in paint, gunpowder, tobacco, and other approved articles of barter in Indian traffic; we also made arrangements for some Indians to attend next day to pilot us up to the village of the Koshkeemo Indians at the eastern extremity of the bay—intending to pass one night there and to put to sea in the morning. We also took this opportunity of replenishing our supply of water, an article universally obtainable, of good quality and in abundance, on the shores of Vancouver. We had to beat for some time against the wind in endeavouring to make the Koshkeemo village. The wind at length failing, we arranged for two of the largest canoes to tow us in—an operation which they successfully accomplished, with the accompaniment of an unceasing chorus of shouting and singing, if their monotonous chanting can be dignified by the latter term. Every now and then they would stop, declaring they were tired, and we could only induce them to proceed by the threat of refusing to keep to our part of the agreement if they failed to perform theirs; we having agreed to pay them in biscuit and molasses for their trouble. At length, after a long, but in no sense of the term either a steady pull or a pull altogether—a thing, indeed, never attempted by the Indians in paddling—we found ourselves anchored off the Koshkeemo village. During all this time we had a very decent, civil sort of an Indian on board, who gave directions as to the course we ought to pursue—together with his wife, who was proud of displaying the little English she knew, which consisted of three words of undoubted practical utility —"Good you give."

On approaching the coast we hove our lead,

which gave first seventeen and a moment afterwards seven fathoms. Being now afraid of going ashore we dropped our anchor, but it did not hold, and on sounding again we got fifteen and then fourteen fathoms, until we at length came-to in a nice spot in about ten fathoms water. Here we waited for some time to receive a visit from the chief of this tribe, but his numerous engagements having, we presume, prevented him from favouring us with his company, we were fain to content ourselves with the polite attention of the sub-chief, who invited us to his hut, taking us on shore in a canoe paddled by himself, his wife, and his daughter. His hut was a good specimen of an Indian hut of the larger size, belonging to a chief. It was about eight or nine feet in height, by about fifty in length and twenty in width. The interior was less encumbered with boxes than is generally the case in Indian dwellings, as this interesting family were in the act of moving when we called upon them, and some portion of their luggage had been sent on before them up the river, preparatory to their migration for the winter or hunting (fur-catching) season. The whole of the movable property of an Indian is packed in boxes, generally of native manufacture—they are very stout and serviceable, and capable of holding from six to twelve pair of blankets. These latter articles are the chief equivalent for wealth in the eyes of an Indian, and his stock of blankets may be looked upon as representing the balance at his bankers. The fire in an Indian hut is generally made in the centre, the smoke escaping through the chinks in the roof, the planking of which is laid on loose, with intervening spaces when the weather is fine, and overlapping each other in bad or wet weather. In spite, however, of any means of egress it may chance to find, there is generally a vast deal more smoke in an Indian hut than is at all agreeable to the eyes and nose of a white man, and I have frequently been obliged to leave after a few minutes' stay, my eyes smarting and blinded with tears. The fire, which is made of wood, serves the double purpose of cooking and warming the apartment in winter. In a hut of the size I am describing there will generally be found several families located, each with its own fire or domestic hearth. On the present occasion, cooking of the most primitive description, and according to the most approved rules of the Indian *cuisine*, was going on, everything being cooked in wooden bowls, in which the water is made to boil by hot stones being dropped into it with a wooden pair of tongs. Having been received with due honour, and motioned to a seat on a platform raised a few inches above the soil, and covered with matting, we proceeded to make ourselves at home. And, truth to say, our entertainer gave us ample grounds for so doing, for, whether in honour of our visit, or on the score of personal cleanliness and comfort, he proceeded to make an impromptu offhand toilet before the assembled company. This consisted simply in changing his shirt, the only garment he wore; before investing himself with the clean one, which he fished out of the depths of a box, he drew our special attention to it as a curious and valuable article of attire. It was a common blue man-of-war's man's shirt, probably received in barter. Our supper consisted of dried salmon, boiled, which would have been greatly improved by the addition of a little salt—as it was we found it somewhat insipid; at the same time we felt in duty bound to eat as much as we could, as the Indians are very sensitive on this point, imagining that you are displeased with them personally if you do not do justice to their cheer. It was a relief to us, however, to find that we were not expected to carry off such portions as we could not eat, according to the custom universally prevalent among the Indians. Our interpreter having explained that it was not the manner of the English to do so, and that the omission of this act implied no discourtesy on our part, our host consented to waive its observance on the present occasion, passing down the remains of our meal to that portion of the household which might be held to represent the "board below the salt." We well remember, some time previous to this, before we had had much experience of Indian life and manners, placing a large bowl of biscuit before a couple of Indians, leaving them to help themselves, which, having done, they coolly carried off the remainder to their canoe. We could ill spare it at the time, but felt that remonstrance would be useless. Another singular trait in Indian character is the air of apathetic indifference they think proper at all times to assume. An Indian conceives it would be *infra dig.* to display any emotion, or anything in fact amounting to interest or curiosity, even under the most exciting circumstances. This phlegm is not a little provoking at times, and I remember feeling considerably nettled, on a previous occasion, at the indifference displayed by a fellow on receiving the gift of a clasp-knife, an article of great value really in the eyes of an Indian. Perceiving that he did not manifest any great degree of pleasure or gratitude on my presenting it to him, I asked him if it was not "hyas klosh ooknok" (very good), to which he replied, with well-feigned indifference, "wake hyas klosh—tenas klosh," meaning that it was very well, but nothing to boast of. I thought this a rather cool way of receiving what was, in fact, a valued gift, but soon found that it is part of an Indian's nature to assume this studied *sang-froid.* The only occasion on which we succeeded in liciting anything like a manifestation of interest and astonishment was when we exhibited the performance of a breech-loading rifle, one of Terry's, having previously submitted its mechanism to their inspection. After several shots their long pent-up wonder and admiration found vent in a deep-drawn "ha!"—at the same time we could understand, from certain remarks that passed among them, that they felt absolute concern and regret that a weapon in all respects so valuable and efficient, should be disfigured by the defect of loading in so unnatural and strange a fashion. Before taking leave of our host of Koshkeemo, I must not forget to mention the vast store of dried salmon, rock-cod and salmon-roe which he had laid up for winter use.

## CHAPTER VI.

Weather changes for the worse—Heavy Rains—Time consumed by Indians in striking a Bargain—Religious Chants—Ancient Carvings—Salmon Weir—We Leave our Anchorage—Heavy Swell at Sea—Dangerous Rocks—Difficult and Hazardous Navigation—Bay of Klaskeeno—Cogwell Trader—Want of Fresh Food—Klaskeeno River—Contrary Winds—Critical Position of our Yacht—Assistance rendered by Indians—Fresh Ballast on Board—Improvement in the Weather—We again put to Sea.

SEVERAL strange canoes came alongside us next day, attracted by the information, conveyed by a canoe we had despatched on our arrival, that there was a ship, with white men on board, lying off Koshkeemo. We purchased a few skins, and tried to engage some Indians to tow us down to the sea on the succeeding morning; before we required their services, however, the weather had changed so much for the worse, that we felt it would be imprudent to leave till it cleared. Instead of improving, however, as the day wore on, it only grew worse, the glass rapidly falling. We could see by the clouds that it was blowing hard, and the swell rolling into the bay conveyed the unpleasant intelligence that there was a heavy sea running outside. Canoes full of Indians kept arriving, on and off, during the day. We were much amused at the way their occupants would sit, for hours at a stretch, placidly gazing at us, apparently wholly indifferent to the pouring rain, which never ceased for one moment. They did not seem so well provided with clothing and blankets as those on the opposite shores of the island. Our attention was here first attracted to that singular Indian custom, which consists, not in flattening, but in elongating the skull, and causing the forehead to recede. This is known as the sugar-loaf-shaped head. Two girls who had been alongside every day since our arrival, had skulls of this shape. This singular deformity is, of course, produced artificially, and is considered a mark of high distinction.

Finding that we were likely to be detained some time, we had made up our minds to a trip up the river that here flows into the Bay, but the continued heavy rain induced us to abandon our design for the present. We managed to procure some fresh salmon—about the last of the season—but could not purchase any rock-cod, which rather surprised us, as we had found plenty at our last anchorage. I am sorry we cannot complimen t our Indian friends on their business habits, but the time they waste in making up their minds to strike a bargain is amazing. At first we found this rather annoying, but at length we got accustomed to it, and allowed them to sit in their canoes, or on our deck, while they turned the weighty matter over in their minds, now exchanging a few remarks among themselves, now relapsing into silence, and thus frequently spending whole hours before they came to a satisfactory conclusion. They were also much in the habit of striking up a monotonous chant as they lay alongside. This chant somewhat resembles those in use in the Roman Catholic Church, and is no doubt an imitation of something they have been taught by the missionaries of that creed. I do not know if these latter ever penetrated thus far, and apprehend that, in most cases, the Indians learn this chant from one another, being given to understand that it is good for them to make use of it. It is very monotonous, consisting of little more than the repetition of the syllables "O sa say, O ma nay!" though not wholly unmusical, especially when heard from a distance, as they accompany themselves in paddling. On one occasion, after they had been chanting, on and off, all day, till late in the afternoon, they were summoned on shore by an old white-haired Indian, who hailed them from the land. On asking one of them where they were going, he made the sign of the cross, but we could not understand what he said.

We observed that the custom of placing the dead among the branches of the trees, is generally practised among these tribes.

The weather cleared up after we had been here about a week, the wind also falling, but the sea still continued too high for us to venture out. We managed to shoot a few duck, and bought some fine geese of the Indians, for two match-boxes of powder each. We thoroughly inspected the Koshkeemo village the same day, especially noticing the quaint carvings with which they decorate their houses, many of them being fixed on the end of poles. They are evidently, in many cases, of great antiquity, being frequently quite discoloured by long exposure to the elements. Many of the principal huts belonging to the chiefs and great men of the tribe, are decorated inside as well as out.

During our stay here we ascended a small river flowing into the south of Koshkeemo inlet, until absolutely hindered from proceeding farther by a cascade, which formed a very picturesque object, dashing over a mass of broken rock. Long before reaching this point, however, we found the course of the stream much impeded by fallen timber. At the entrance or mouth of this little river we always had to steer clear of a number of stakes; these, being interlaced with slips of bark, formed a salmon weir, which, while affording ingress to the salmon at one particular spot, prevent their finding their way out, unless they happen to strike that same spot again. Salmon are also frequently taken by the Indians, in baskets of their own construction. The crows, which we everywhere observed feeding on the offal thrown out by the Indians on the beach, appear to be held in some reverence by them; at least they never kill these birds themselves, and do not like to see a white man shoot them. This regard for the crow may probably be connected with the superstition of Yale, to which we have already alluded.

We had now been detained some ten days in Quatsinough Harbour, and we had fully made up our minds to diversify the monotony of our sojourn by walking across the island along the Indian trail to Fort Rupert. Just as we were about to carry this plan into execution, however, the weather fortunately moderated, and we at once prepared to quit our anchorage, of which we had become heartily weary. We were towed out as far as the open sea by an Indian canoe, and took one of its crew on board as a pilot, being ignorant of this part of the coast, paying the remainder in tobacco for their services. We found a very heavy swell outside, with but little wind, consequently we rolled about a good deal. After some time we were overtaken by a squall, which, though it did not last, took us along some distance on our course. We had no more wind till the afternoon, but the sea was still very high, and our progress, consequently, difficult. Towards nightfall we could hear the sea breaking in thunder on a reef of rocks on our lee, and dark as it was getting, it being by this time past five, we could distinguish the white line of breakers. Our position was evidently a critical one, as we became gradually convinced that we had rocks on all sides of us, none of which could we find marked on the chart we were provided with; we were, in fact, running through a perfect archipelago of rocks. Our Indian, though pretty confident at first, eventually declared he did not know where he was. The peculiar roll of the sea soon convinced us we were getting into shallow water. We sounded, and got, first ten, then seven and six fathoms, and at length found ourselves in the midst of a dense bed of kelp, which was by no means reassuring. Fortunately, however, the moon now began to show from behind a lofty ridge of hill, and great as was our danger we could not forbear admiring the terrible grandeur of the scene her light revealed. On every one of the different reefs of rock by which we were beset, the giant swell of the Pacific was bursting in cataracts of foam, flinging up columns of snowy spray into the midnight air. The hollow thunder of the breakers coming to us from some quarter or other, was never out of our ears the whole of this night of toil and danger. On emerging from the bed of kelp in which we were some time involved, we had to steer our course with the utmost care and vigilance, scarcely ever being on the same tack for ten minutes together. The weather had now become very cold, and we only contrived to keep ourselves warm and fit for work by supplies of hot coffee at frequent intervals throughout the night. It was only towards morning that we found ourselves fairly out of danger, and making for the Bay of Klaskeeno.

Daylight revealed to us some of the dangers we had just escaped; the entrance to this bay being approached through the midst of a number of sunken and other rocks, is very ticklish navigation, especially at night. I will not weary the reader further by describing the labyrinth of rocks we had to thread ere we could find a secure anchorage; suffice it to say we at length found a likely spot, in which we dropped our anchor.

On going on shore we observed the first traces we had seen of frost on the grass—it was now the 2nd of November. We received the usual visits from Indians in their canoes, and among others we noticed a Cogwell trader from Fort Rupert, who had travelled overland by the Indian track we spoke of, to Quatsinough, and from there on to this place in his canoe. He agreed to take our pilot back with him on his return; we also entrusted him with a letter to our friend Willie Mitchell, the chief trader at Fort Rupert, informing him that we had been safely inside Quatsinough Harbour during the recent gales. We tried to engage an Indian to pilot us to the next village, but he refused to come, on account of the unsettled state of the weather—promising, however, to do so as soon as it should moderate. Finding this did not take place for two or three days, he refused to have anything more to do with us, no doubt setting us down as unlucky. We were greatly disappointed at finding the Indians were unable to supply us with anything in the way of fresh food, of which we stood greatly in need, they living entirely on dried salmon, or on sea-birds of an intolerable fishy flavour. We at length succeeded in procuring a few domestic fowl's eggs, which proved a real luxury.

The weather continued rainy, with heavy squalls, for several days longer, and we were therefore detained here watching the sea break on the rocks outside the harbour. Being out of coal, we were obliged to take wood on board as fuel.

On the third day the weather moderated, but there was still too much sea for a canoe to venture out of the harbour. We pulled some distance up the Klaskeeno River; it is a fine broad stream, very deep in places, and flowing between lofty ridges of pine-covered mountains. I shot a few herons, and noticed a number of shag about, a bird well known on the Cornish coast. We observed Indians using the bow and arrow in shooting birds. Going ashore on a point of the bay one morning, we saw the naked beams of the summer residence of the Indians; we shot a few stock-duck, the very best eating of any description of duck, and from time to time procured a few wild fowl from the Indians; but, truth to say, our supplies were falling very short, vegetables we had none left, we were therefore very anxious to get away.

On the tenth day of our stay here, the weather having moderated somewhat, we resolved to make a start, although entirely against the advice of the Indians, and got fairly away. An hour saw us clear of the rocks at the entrance. Outside this we found the wind blowing from the southeast, in a contrary direction to the wind inside the bay. We tried for some time to make head against it, but the sea was so heavy that we found it impossible, so wore ship and ran in for the rocks once more. We now met the wind blowing straight out of the bay. This singular anomaly was no doubt due to the peculiar conformation of the coast, the wind drawing through the mountains and rushing down as if out of a funnel. We had therefore to beat up for our former anchorage. At one moment we were placed in the most critical position a vessel can be in. Just as we were going round, on a fresh tack, close to some rocks, on which a heavy sea was breaking, the wind entirely died away, and we were becalmed for a few seconds. In this hazardous position a sudden gust seized us, and we had the narrowest escape in the world of being capsized. At one moment we thought our fate was sealed, but she righted the moment the jib-sheet was let go, and the danger passed away as quickly as it came; everything below however was sent to leeward, as we were at one time considerably below our bearings. During this tempestuous weather, every one on board was accustomed to keep his boots unlaced, ready to kick off at a moment's notice, in the event of our vessel capsizing, so as to have a better chance, if any should exist, of saving his life by swimming. We had a man at each sheet, standing by to let go at once, if necessary. Our hatches were of course battened down, while we ourselves were, one and all, drenched to the skin, not merely by the occasional seas that broke over us, but by the pitiless pelting rain, which never ceased during the whole period of our struggle with the elements. Our narrow escape showed us, among other things, that we were too light in the water, and we registered a vow that, if ever we reached an anchorage again, we would put some more ballast on board. After much trouble and labour in beating up against a succession of wild squalls, accompanied by a deluge of rain, and keeping with some difficulty clear of rocks where the bay narrows, we at length made comparatively smooth waters, thoroughly wet, weary, and dispirited at being thus baffled in our efforts to leave a place where we had already been detained a fortnight.

We were still some considerable distance from our anchorage ground, when we were much pleased to see one of the largest-sized canoes approaching us, its crew keeping time to the beat of their paddles with their religious chant. On coming alongside, they all declared that for some time they had made up their minds that we must be lost. They reproached us for not having followed their advice, saying that the red man understood the elements better than the white man, at the same time offering to take us in tow, for which purpose, indeed, they had put off on seeing us return. We were only too glad to avail ourselves of their services, and taking all sail off our craft, we threw them a couple of tow-lines, and in due time brought up at our old anchorage, when we did not fail to acknowledge the kindness of the chief who had sent us this timely assistance, or to reward the crew who had so ably carried out his intentions.

We were thus compelled to lie here for three days longer, our provisions being by this time so greatly reduced, that oatmeal porridge constituted our breakfast, and Indian dried salmon the staple of our dinner. Of course, we did not venture to touch the reserve of salt meat we kept in store as a provision against the eventuality of being blown out to sea at any future time. Early the next morning we acted on the experience for which we had nearly paid so dear the day before—we got a ton and a half, or two tons, of stone on board; it is one thing, however, to get stone on board, but quite another to stow ballast, especially under the present trying circumstances, and it cost us no small amount of time and labour to get everything snug and ship-shape below. The next day being fine, we devoted some more time to getting our little craft in what we considered good sailing trim, and got our sails up to dry. Towards evening my aneroid barometer, in which I place implicit confidence, stood very high, from $29\frac{9}{10}°$ to $30°$. We spent some time endeavouring to get a shot at something to replenish our larder, but only succeeded in knocking over one duck. The next day saw us once again at sea, riding the waves of the Pacific. Getting sight of the sun, I was enabled to ascertain that we were in latitude $50°\ 3'$ north. This discovery was highly satisfactory to all on board, as it proved that we were at length some three miles to the south of the long talked-of "Woody Point," which we had hoped to reach nearly a month earlier.

## CHAPTER VII.

Heavy Seas after Recent Gales—Freshsets from the Coast—Mocuina Point—Escalante Reef—We drift out to Sea—Thick Fog—Make Friendly Cove—Nootka Sound—Strange Sail on the Horizon—Indians come alongside—Cooptee, Winter Quarters of the Mowichats—Noise made over a Kluquolla—Mocoola, Chief of the Mowichats—Takes a Fancy to our Dog—Indian Opinion of European Garments—Pe-Sha-Klim, Spouter of the Mowichats—Indian Presents—Tomahawk and other Arms—Narrative of an Adventure on our Former Visit—We ascend Guaquina Arm—Hostility of the Matchclats—Indian War-whoop—They fire on us—We parley with them—Peace Restored—We go on Shore with the Chief—Encampment—Fresh Symptoms of Hostility—Satisfactory Explanations—Fail to reach the Object of our Expedition—Arrival of Pe-Sha-Klim.

The first two days at sea we found the rolling swell left by the late tempestuous weather very troublesome, especially on the second, as the wind entirely failed us. Though by no means anxious to be too near in shore, as, in the event of a south-east wind springing up, we should have had great difficulty in standing clear, we did not bargain to be carried out as far as eighteen or twenty miles, reducing the appearance of land to a mere blue ridge in the distance. This was no doubt caused by the freshsets, issuing from the various arms of the sea in Nootka Sound, and finding an exit in Esperanza Inlet. As all things must have an end, on the third day we got a nice breeze from the westward, and, as the moon changed, we hoped to have kept it all day. No such luck, however, was in store for us, and towards evening we found ourselves close to Mocuina Point, at the entrance to Nootka Sound. Could I have foreseen the weather that was reserved for us, I should have endeavoured to make the harbour that night. As it came on very dark, however, and none of us being very well acquainted with the navigation of these waters, I deemed it more prudent to lay to and await daylight. Scarcely had we turned in, hoping to make ourselves comfortable for the night, when the gradually increasing motion of the vessel, and the rattle and clatter of the cordage, told us unmistakably that the wind was getting up, and sure enough from about one till four a.m. it blew half a gale. The proximity of Escalante Reef to leeward would alone have been sufficient to keep us awake and watchful, if the violent pitching to which we were subjected had not produced this effect. As the sun rose the wind went down, and we found we had drifted considerably out to sea. This must have been caused in a great measure by the combined action of the sea and tide, after the wind failed, which was the case about five in the morning, though a tremendous sea was still running. About nine, a slight breeze springing up, we had some hopes of getting round the Point by midday. The wind, however, proved light and we drifted to the northward, the tide setting us up in that direction, and about one p.m. we were fast approaching the Bajo Reef, a very ugly ledge of rock running out from Nootka Island, to which I shall have occasion to draw the attention of my readers hereafter. I will not now, therefore, tax their patience by relating the difficulties we had to contend with on the present occasion. After taking turns at the sweeps at intervals, we got a breeze from the southward and westward, and were enabled to make a fair wind of it about nine at night. As a very thick fog came up, we kept her close round the rocks, leading into Friendly Cove, Nootka Sound. We ran her round the point into Friendly Cove just as the fog was at its thickest, and got our anchor down about ten p.m., all on board being very glad to exchange a sea-watch for an anchor-watch. As we could see neither fire nor light of any kind on shore when the fog lifted, we felt sure that the Indians had left their village at Mocuina.

Early in the morning we fired our swivel gun to attract the attention of any Indians who might be cruising about, as we were desirous of ascertaining where the Mowichats, inhabiting this shore of Nootka Sound, were then located.

Proceeding on shore we rambled through the now deserted Indian village, and making our way over the rocks above, we at length reached the shores of the Pacific. Great was our astonishment, on sighting the ocean again, to behold the unwonted spectacle of a sail on the horizon. We were lost in conjecture as to what vessel could be cruising in these waters at this season of the year, nor did our glass, which we soon brought to bear upon her, at all assist us in arriving at anything like a satisfactory conclusion. We made her out indeed to be a two-masted vessel, but were thoroughly mystified by the nondescript character of her rig, and were almost disposed, while laughing at the absurdity of the idea, to set her down as a Chinese junk of the largest size.

While employed in gathering a crop of fresh greens, in the shape of turnip-tops, the wild progeny of some that had been sown years before by the Spaniards, we were recalled to our vessel by two shots, fired from the swivel gun, the preconcerted signal of the approach of Indians. Hastening on board, we found that our gun of the morning had been heard, and that the Indians had come from some distance up the Sound, fully expecting to find us in our present anchorage of **Friendly Cove.** Getting under weigh we managed, by dint of alternately sailing and being towed, to reach the winter quarters of the Mowichats, Cooptee. We were now no longer "en pays de connaissance," although still among tribes of whom we had had some previous acquaintance—this being our second visit to Nootka Sound. The first night we passed off the village was disturbed by the shouts and uproar of the Indians, who were engaged in the important ceremony of creating a Kluquolla. I have already alluded to the various rites practised on these occasions.

Early the next morning, the chief of the Mowichats and his wife came off to pay us a visit. Of course it was merely a case of renewing a former acquaintance between ourselves and Mocoola, as the chief of the Mowichats is called. Captain Cook, on the occasion of his visit to Nootka Sound, speaks of the then chief of this tribe by the same name. After an interchange of mutual civilities, Mocoola and his spouse seemed to find great pleasure in drawing my attention to a couple of gold rings, of which I had formerly made them a present, and which they still displayed on their fingers. The chief of the Mowichats himself also again condescended to notice my little four-footed companion, a thorough-bred bull-dog, of very small size, which I had brought with me from England, and which had greatly taken his fancy on the occasion of my first visit. So anxious, indeed, was he to become possessed of it, that he had proposed to me to exchange it for an animal of his own breeding, a vile mongrel, of the most worthless description. I unhesitatingly refused to do anything of the sort, at the same time, with a view of consoling him to some extent for the disappointment, I determined to make him a present of some article of clothing, and, on rummaging my wardrobe, found I could best spare a pair of trowsers, which I accordingly presented to him, with all due ceremony, hoping he might be induced to regard them as an article of state attire, to be worn on high-days and holidays. In this, however, I was grievously disappointed, as my gift found no favour in his eyes, nor did the fact of their having been cut by Hill, of Bond Street, constitute any additional recommendation. He declared them to be vain and foolish inventions of the white man for impeding free locomotion, and actually returned them to me as worthless, after having first cut off all the buttons, the only thing about them to which he attached any value!

It is not, however, so much to the chief of the Mowichats himself, as to his herald, or spouter, that I would direct the reader's attention, and whom I forthwith beg to introduce as a friend, whose acquaintance we all had great pleasure in renewing, and who, we believe, fully reciprocated our feelings. Pe Sha Klim, as he called himself, was a thoroughly good-natured, and, in his savage fashion, good-hearted fellow. In person he was stalwart and robust, his expression was good-tempered and agreeable, his countenance being lighted up by a frequent smile, displaying a good set of teeth. At times, however, I am bound to confess that I have seen, when engaged in an excited discussion with his fellows, the true fire of the savage flash into his eye, and give animation to his gestures. The title of "Scokum tum-tum Siwash," or, "Strong-hearted Savage," which he was much given to insist upon as being one of his special designations, has often seemed to me not inaptly to describe him. Being the herald, or spouter, of the chief of the Mowichats, whose office it is to deliver messages and proclaim orders in the loudest possible tone of voice, supplying the want of a speaking trumpet by force of lungs, he was of course selected for the strength and quality of those organs. The way in which he would sing out any announcement from the chief was quite startling, when heard for the first time, and we have frequently caught the deep tones of his voice, floating over the still waters of the bay, from an almost incredible distance. He was commonly in the habit of shouting his orders to his men on shore, from the deck of our cutter, at a distance of at least five to six hundred yards.

We went through the ceremony of receiving presents from our various Indian acquaintance, a fine black bear skin being sent us from Mocoola, which unfortunately was not dry enough for us to take away. The sub-chief of the Mowichats was a very cross-grained, churlish sort of a fellow, and having on a previous occasion had experience of his disagreeable temper, we kept studiously aloof from him, hoping he would abstain from making us any present, as we should not then be called upon to make any return; for receiving presents from Indians is merely another name for barter, an equivalent in return being in every case expected. There was no help for it, however, as he, in turn, came off in his canoe, and deposited his gift, a land otter, on our decks. Some few hours afterwards we sent him what we deemed a suitable recompense; being, however, it would appear, of a different opinion himself, he again came alongside, and, after bitterly reproaching us with our niggardly spirit, to our great amusement walked off with the present he had lately made us, and which was still lying on the deck, keeping, at the same time, what we had given him in return. We were, however, glad to get rid of him even at this price.

Going ashore with our friend Pe Sha Klim, who, be it known to the reader, was the warlike representative of a line of ancestors illustrious for deeds of arms, he invited me to his tent, and displayed a number of arms and trophies that had descended to him as heirlooms, and of which he was not a little proud. Among these, my attention was especially drawn to a tomahawk of great age, which had evidently seen no inconsiderable share of service. The handle was a massive club of hard wood, carved in the usual manner, into which the hatchet or cutting part, consisting of the point of an old whale harpoon, was inserted. The head of the animal it was carved to represent was decorated with a fringe or mane of human hair, taken from the heads of the different foemen who had bitten the dust before it, and in which I could plainly distinguish hair of different colours. Pe Sha Klim expressed a confident opinion that the result of his prowess in battle would be to add very considerably to the length of the mane. I made various offers to induce the Mowichat warrior to part with this trophy of savage life, on this and subsequent occasions, but without success.

His hut was decorated with arms of various descriptions, old bows and arrows, knives made of files stolen from the Hudson's Bay Company, and an old blunderbuss; in addition to these he possessed the usual musket carried by Indians generally.

On the occasion of my former visit to Nootka Sound during the summer, when the village of the

Mowichats is at Friendly Cove, I had determined to extend my trip by a visit to the Matchelat Indians, whose village is situated at the extremity of one of the arms communicating with the Sound. We started on this expedition one fine day in August, and I will briefly interrupt the course of my narrative while I relate what befell us on the occasion of this visit. The Matchelats, to whom I am about to introduce the reader, are a tribe constantly at war with the Mowichats; the origin of the feud being, I believe, of recent date, arising as far as I could understand, out of the treacherous murder of the late chief of the Mowichats by the Matchelats, when the former, in company with a few young warriors, was up the country exploring for gold-dust.

We were much impressed during this cruise by the natural beauties of Nootka Sound. Every point we doubled would display a fresh panorama of pine-covered mountain and rock, with occasional vistas opening far up into the interior, and revealing distant peaks of greater altitude still; while the blue, unruffled surface of the bay was dotted with innumerable islands, sometimes of naked rock, sometimes feathered down to the water's edge with mingled foliage of various tints. We are now speaking of the month of August. On entering Gua-quina arm, steep ridges of mountain, densely covered with pine, shut in the view on either hand.

I ought here to mention that we had an Indian on board, who had accidentally become one of our crew; the breeze having suddenly freshened so much when he was on board our vessel some few days before, that he had cast off his canoe and left his companion to take it ashore, while he remained to barter, we having agreed to take him with us and land him among some friendly tribes further south. Proceeding up Guaquina arm, we had to anchor the first night amidst a group of small rocky islets. Next morning we went on shore and ascended an eminence, commanding an extensive prospect, with the design of reconnoitring the country. From this point we perceived a canoe in the distance, which we eagerly hailed, as we were ignorant of the locality, and did not know how far it was to the village of the Matchelats. Finding they did not perceive us, we fired a gun and sent on one of our crew with the Indian in the dingy, to board the canoe. They turned out to be Mowichats, a man and his wife, who told us that the Matchelats had mistaken us for a large northern, and consequently hostile canoe, and had retreated up the sound; we did not altogether credit this account, and struck a bargain to be taken up the river in the canoe, leaving orders for the yacht to follow. The tide being at first against us we kept in shore, and after a short time, coming on a small island, I landed, and as the sun was very hot, enjoyed the luxury of a bath.

Proceeding on our course I frequently made use of a double-barrelled field-glass I carried with me. The attention of our Indian being drawn to this object, I showed him how to use it. He was undoubtedly much astonished at the result, although the remarks he made upon it were by no means flattering. He evidently regarded it as an uncanny, if not absolutely diabolical contrivance for getting an unfair advantage over nature, and returned us our "lying glass," as he expressively termed it, with unmistakable marks of disapprobation. In a short time we perceived a canoe in the distance, the crew of which, on a nearer approach, treated my ears for the first time to a genuine Indian war-whoop. Our crew answered them by a friendly shout, which was at length returned. They wanted to know who we were and what we were doing there, and were answered that we were a party of white men who had come in a vessel of our own to visit them, with friendly intentions. The canoe was still too far from us to distinguish the number on board. They now disappeared for a short time round a point; on again sighting them, however, we pulled towards them, on which they repeated their war-whoop, our party again answering with a friendly shout. They now made for the shore, and pulled round a point, we still continuing to approach them. In a few moments we saw a number of naked figures with muskets in their hands, dodging about among the trees on the point, and on taking a survey of them with our glass, we could perceive the heads of many others just showing over the rocks in every direction, their faces and hands being painted black, in token of war. In another moment the sharp report of a number of muskets awoke the echoes of the rocky shores around us. Not knowing what it meant, we continued to pull towards them, when they again opened fire, and this time the whistle of a number of balls about our ears afforded unequivocal proof that they meant something more than frightening us. Matters now looked serious; we were evidently in a very critical position; at the same time, feeling it was the best policy to put a bold face on the affair, we opened a parley with them, our Mowichat being spokesman. They declared, however, that he had deceived them before, and they would not now believe a word he said. The tide, meanwhile, having turned, was setting us in shore towards them. They now sent a charge of swan-shot at us to make us bring up, we still continuing to parley with them, but at the same time backing water to keep out of their reach, as the shot they had just fired ploughed up the water on all sides of us. We informed them that our interpreter, well known to them by name, he having been in the habit of visiting these coasts for the last eight years, was on board. They replied however, that he had been bribed by the Mowichats to deceive them, adding, at the same time, "You must not think to steal a march upon us in the day time; we are fully prepared for you." Meanwhile, keeping a sharp eye on them, I saw one man stoop down and, resting his musket on a stone, take deliberate aim at us. Thinking it decidedly too warm to be pleasant, I ordered the canoe to turn back. Perceiving this, the Indians said, "If the interpreter," naming him, "is really on board, let him come on shore." But our Mowichat replied, "No; you have too many muskets, and are firing ball—he won't come." We were not informed of this reply at the time, but he was afraid that, if we landed, the Matchelats would be sure to kill our poor Esquihat Indian. We therefore paddled away from them, telling them to put off to us in a canoe if they were friendly and wished to hold further parley with us. Continuing to increase the distance between us, we at length beheld them push off in a canoe, and a few minutes after were much gratified to see our yacht coming down with the tide in good style.

The Indians, on perceiving our vessel, evidently felt great doubt and uneasiness as to the course they ought to pursue. They probably expected us to take summary vengeance on them for having fired on us. As we continued, however, to assure them that our intentions were friendly, they at length mustered sufficient courage to come alongside, but were thrown into a state of considerable consternation on learning from our interpreter that I was " Man-of-war Tyhee," and highly indignant at being fired on, as we had done nothing to provoke a misunderstanding, and they could have had no reason to doubt our good faith. We insisted on one of their warriors coming on board; at the same time I gave orders to have the big gun loaded with grape, with ten or twelve more rounds ready for her if required, and had all the small arms ranged on deck, with about thirty rounds to each. Having thus completed our armament and prepared for the worst, we ran up the ensign and steered direct for the point from which we had been fired on. The Indians on shore, as we could now perceive, had dropped their muskets, their companion on board telling them that we were prepared for them now, and would soon make it too hot for them if they ventured on any further hostile demonstration. When we were well round the point, I informed them that their chief might come on board, but that they must first give proof of their friendly intentions by firing off their muskets; this they showed they had already done by snapping the locks. The chief shortly afterwards came on board, and our interpreter demanded of him if he wanted peace: he replied "Yes," on which I ordered the small arms below, and gave him a present of some biscuit. He afterwards sent a deer on board, which we found very acceptable, having had no fresh meat since we were at the Esquihat village some weeks before.

Peace having been, as we hoped, thus definitively concluded, I went on shore with the chief. Being desirous of carrying out my original intention of visiting the Matchelat village, I requested him to lend us his aid in carrying out our design. This he promised to do, and we agreed to accompany him to the encampment of the Matchelats, six miles up the river, to sleep there that night, and to go up to the village the next morning. By showing that we placed implicit confidence in the Indians themselves, we hoped to inspire them with a similar feeling, and taking, therefore, a stock of provisions with us, we started on our expedition. On our way up the river, we landed at a stockade of Indian construction, in a very dilapidated condition however. Our chief, nevertheless, seemed very proud of it, and fully confident in its capacity for resisting a siege, as he informed us that he intended to retire into it in case of an attack from any of his enemies. Proceeding on our journey we at length reached the Indian encampment, situated in a very sheltered and secluded spot, evidently chosen with a view to concealing themselves, as we should never have dreamt of looking for an encampment in such a spot. Before bivouacking for the night, I took a ramble through the woods, or rather, to speak more accurately, a scramble up the rocky pine-clad slope, at the foot of which our encampment lay, and from various points of which I obtained some views of the surrounding scenery, of an equally wild character, together with occasional glimpses of the distant windings of the river. I ought not to forget to mention that I was accompanied by a couple of Indians, and having my revolver with me, a weapon in which they evidently felt great interest and curiosity, I fired four barrels in quick succession at a mark on a tree, by way of illustrating its mechanism and mode of action. The gathering shades of evening warning us to return, I perceived, on again approaching our encampment, fresh symptoms either of hostility or suspicion on the part of the Indians, several of whom, with muskets in their hands, were lurking among the trunks of the trees. Sending one of our Indian companions forward to inquire if there was anything the matter, the mystery was soon cleared up. It appears that, on hearing the different shots I fired from my revolver, they conceived the idea that I had inveigled their comrades into the woods and there murdered them. Finding how entirely erroneous all their suspicions had been, we were soon the best of friends again, and, to increase their good-will towards us, we distributed the whole of our stock of biscuit among them, a piece of generosity of which we repented afterwards, as we had nothing but dried fish to eat for the rest of our trip. During the night we spent with the Matchclats, it appears that a large tree fell close alongside the encampment. The noise it made, crashing through the underwood, aroused everyone in the camp except myself, for being very tired I slept very soundly. On returning when the danger was over, the Indians were very much surprised to see me still asleep, or at most only just aroused, and still unaware of the cause of the unusual commotion in the camp. Inquiring of the interpreter how it happened that I was so apparently indifferent to imminent danger, the former took advantage of the circumstance, wholly without my cognizance or sanction however, to impress them with a belief that I was endowed with supernatural attributes, saying that I slept in no dread of a tree falling on me, or any other danger threatening me, as I possessed the power of averting all such catastrophes, and no tree could possibly fall on the spot I had selected for my couch without my express knowledge and permission. Whatever may be thought of our interpreter's ruse, it certainly had the effect of wonderfully increasing the deference and respect shown to me by these simple children of nature during the remainder of my sojourn among them.

Whether the chief of the Matchclats now began to fear any possible influence so great a chief, as I had suddenly grown in their eyes, might acquire over his followers and dependents if I reached their head-quarters, or whether he was still suspicious that we were but enemies in disguise, certain it is he, from this time, persisted in throwing every possible obstacle in the way of our projected visit to the Matchelat village. Excuse followed excuse, and delay followed delay; there was declared to be too little water in the Guaquina arm or river for the canoes to ascend thus far, until at length, knowing the hopeless obstinacy of Indian character, and the impossibility of shaking their fixed and settled resolution, we reluctantly abandoned our project, and returned on board the "Templar," our yacht.

Having spent the night on board, we were informed the next morning that there was a strange canoe in the distance. This turned out to contain a party of Mowichat warriors, under the command of our friend Pe Sha Klim, whose suspicions were aroused by the long absence of the Mowichat Indian, in whose canoe, it will be remembered, we had originally been fired on, and they had therefore put out in search of their missing kinsman, prepared to avenge his death in case of foul play on the part of the Matchelats. In anticipation of war, therefore, they had left their women in a place of safety round a point, it being the universal custom among Indians to put the women out of harm's way when they think danger imminent.

## CHAPTER VIII.

The Wreck of the "Florentia"—Sufferings of the Crew—Resolution Cove—Perilous Adventure in an Open Boat—Bocca del Inferno—Misunderstanding between the Shipwrecked Crew and the Indians—Dress of an Indian Woman—The Use of Paint—Primitive *Poste-Restante*—Captain Cook.

WE will now once more resume the thread of our present narrative, which, it will be remembered, we quitted at Cooptee, the winter quarters of the Mowichats, it being by this time the 25th of November. We got under weigh on the morning of that day about half-past five. A fair breeze soon took us out abreast the Escalante Reef, on passing which, however, the wind failed us. About midday we again fancied we made out something like a sail in the distance, and eventually, with the aid of our glass, we discovered her to be the same two-masted craft we had already sighted, and our curiosity was once more thoroughly aroused. About half-past one we perceived something coming towards us, which we at first supposed to be a boat, but which turned out to be a canoe. On coming alongside her Indian crew informed us that the vessel whose singular appearance had caused so much interest and speculation on board our cutter was a large craft, water-logged, and in other respects a perfect wreck, and having King George's (English) men on board, who were short of food and water. The additional stimulus of a desire to aid our fellow-countrymen in distress being now added to the curiosity we had from the first felt to know what vessel she could be, we resolved to try and board her.

A wind from the south-east springing up, we beat our vessel in a vain endeavour to approach her until near eight in the evening, when we found we could get no nearer. A canoe now put off from her, and we sent back all the food we could spare, being unfortunately very short ourselves just now, together with a good stock of fresh water, and also a note, saying we would try and make her in the morning. This we endeavoured for a long time to do, until, being at length again baffled, we were obliged to return to Friendly Cove about ten A.M.

Next morning as we were going on shore to try and get some geese, we saw the ship herself coming up the Sound. We fired our gun and displayed a red ensign from a commanding point of rock to attract the attention of those on board her. Failing, however, to do so, we got under weigh, and after a troublesome beat, the wind coming down in tremendous puffs, we at length got so near her that two of our number put off in the small boat to go on board. She proved to be the "Florentia," of Callao, bound for that port from Victoria, with a cargo of timber. The crew turned out to be Americans, not Englishmen, it being a ruse on their part to describe themselves as "King George's men" to the Indians, in order to secure their good services, as had the latter been aware that they were "Boston men,"—the name by which all Americans of the United States are indiscriminately known among Indians—they would have been more likely to meet with ill-treatment than assistance, such is the hatred borne by the Indian races to the "Boston man."

The story of their shipwreck was one of those touching narratives of suffering, toil, and danger that so often form a terrible yet thrilling episode in the lives of those whose destiny is cast upon the mighty waters.

She had capsized at sea in a gale of wind fifty miles south of Cape Flattery, just that day fortnight, it being now the 26th of November, consequently the very same day as that on which we were so nearly capsized ourselves on attempting to leave Klaskeeno. The captain, supercargo, and

I

a Dr. Baillie of Victoria, a passenger, perished by drowning. The remainder of the crew managed to cling to the wreck, owing their preservation from certain destruction solely to the fact of her being timber-laden, and therefore incapable of sinking. After a time she righted, but was, of course, completely water-logged, and sunk to the water's edge, every swell sweeping her deck. The unhappy survivors found themselves, therefore, in possession of existence truly, but under circumstances which, in the eyes of most men, would seem to render it hardly endurable. Drenched to the skin, almost without food, entirely without fresh water, without warmth, shelter, or comfort of any kind, in a water-logged and nigh unmanageable craft, on a part of the ocean where there was barely the remotest chance of their attracting the attention of any vessel, their case did indeed seem desperate. At first it appeared as if death must inevitably, in a few days, put an end to their sufferings. That they survived to tell the story of their adventures is a signal proof that men should never lose heart, even when things seem at their worst, but trusting in Providence, resolutely, and at once, strive to set them right again. "*Nil desperandum*" is pre-eminently the motto of the seaman.

By dint of labour and perseverance, they contrived, when the weather moderated, to knock up a rude shed of loose planks on the most elevated portion of the wreck, which afforded them a tolerable shelter. Without being a smoker myself, the narrative of the crew of the " Florentia " has convinced me that the use of tobacco, under certain circumstances, may be not without its advantages, as they undoubtedly owed the preservation of their existence to the fact of one of their number having in his pocket a tin, and therefore water-proof, box of lucifer matches, which he used for lighting his pipe. They were thus enabled to kindle a fire; and another of the crew, who deserves infinite credit for his ingenuity and mechanical skill, managed, with the aid of a few feet of lead pipe, to construct an apparatus for distilling fresh water from the salt sea-water. The quantity thus provided was but small it is true, yet, by careful husbanding, it proved sufficient for their wants; at all events, it enabled them to preserve life.

The " Florentia " must originally have been a very handsome craft, a brig of about 400 tons. As we saw her she was of course a complete wreck, sunk to the water's edge; her deck cabin was gone —everything in fact had been swept away; her lower masts and the mere stump of her bowsprit alone remained standing. The crew had extemporised a fore-sail out of a foretop-sail, and this, with a stay-sail, was all the canvas she carried. Some remnants of other sails, hanging from the shrouds, were beaten by the elements into mere rags, resembling wet tow. The crew were huddled together in the shed they had erected for themselves, and in which they had contrived constantly to keep their fire burning. Being very short of food, they were very grateful, poor fellows, for the trifling assistance we were able to afford them, especially for a bag of potatoes we had sent on board the day before. From the account given of us by the Esquihat Indians, who had been our messengers on that occasion, they expected to find our vessel one of the launches of a man-of-war. Being accustomed to wear the jacket of the Thames Yacht Club, with its brass buttons, to which I sometimes added, when it was blowing, on account of its weight, an old cavalry cap, with its gold band, I always passed in this nondescript costume for a man-of-war Tyhee, or officer, among the Indians of these coasts. The blue ensign of the Thames Yacht Club, which we flew at the peak, no doubt tended to confirm them in this impression, as it differed entirely from anything they had seen in use among trading vessels.

We ran that night into Resolution Cove—thus named by Captain Cook, after his own ship, if I remember right—promising to come and see the crew of the "Florentia" again next day, if they were unable to follow us During the night it blew hard, and we felt no small anxiety for the fate of our friends on the "Florentia." On searching for her the next morning we could discover no traces of her in any direction; I therefore set out in our little boat, accompanied by a friend and one other hand to try and find her. I always used the paddle in preference to the oar in these waters, having by this time become thoroughly expert in handling it; I could thus see where we were going, and steer our craft accordingly. We paddled round the island, between which and the mainland the channel known as Zuciarte Arm runs. Here we found it very hard work against the tide. It rained all day. We could see nothing of the ship, and only sighted one canoe. On rounding the island opposite Friendly Cove we met a tremendous sea rolling in from the Pacific, much more than was agreeable in so small a boat. She was, happily, very buoyant; but we more than once began to think we should never see our yacht again, and it soon became apparent that we were in truth paddling for very life. The entrance to Nootka Sound, as I have before mentioned, is full of rocky islets, on which the sea was now breaking with terrific violence. We had hard work to keep her clear of them, every now and then a gust would come down on us with a fury that made us bow to the gunwale, lest it should capsize us; but our little boat rode the waves gallantly, and at length, after working as men work when their lives are at stake, we succeeded in reaching the "Templar" once more.

Early the next day Pe Sha Klim, and seven other Mowichats, came alongside to inquire after the "Florentia," and shortly after a canoe of Clayoquot Indians arrived on the same errand. This solicitude and anxiety respecting the fate of the vessel, displayed by the Indians, arose no doubt from the fact that the moment a vessel goes on shore they regard her as their legitimate spoil; as a special gift of Providence, in fact, to the poor Indian. At the same time we must do them the justice to say that they are generally willing to lend all the assistance in their power to a vessel in distress, so long as she holds to her anchors. Some years ago a ship of the Hudson's Bay Company, in charge of our friend Willie Mitchell, having been, as he himself informed us, driven ashore in Neah Bay, she was, in spite of his most strenuous efforts to prevent it, stripped of her copper and other valuables, and then burnt.

The next morning a canoe brought us a letter from on board the "Florentia," informing us that she was safely at anchor, and telling us where to find her. We at once set sail, making the Indians come on board, and taking their canoe in tow. Soon after we cleared the point round which Resolution Cove is situated, we sighted the masts of the ship. We made for her, but the wind failing and the tide running down, we put into a small cove in which the Indians reported there was good anchorage. We were about to let go our anchor, when, seeing the rocks very distinctly under the water, we hesitated, and ultimately dropped it in another spot; it was lucky we did so, as these rocks were left quite dry at low water, the tide having fallen two and a quarter fathoms since we entered the cove.

On going on board the "Florentia" we found her crew very much more comfortable; they had roofed in the house on deck, and were endeavouring to pump her dry with the assistance of the Indians. They informed us that she had drifted during the night, but that her anchors had at length brought her up in that spot.

The next day we paid a visit to the "Bocca del Inferno," thus named by the Spaniards in consequence of the violence with which the tide ebbs and flows through its narrow rocky entrance. When once inside, we found ourselves in a land-locked basin of considerable extent.

One morning, while still at anchor, being detained by the wind, which continued obstinately in the south-east, Pe Sha Klim came alongside, and we were not long in remarking from his manner that there was something amiss. On coming on deck he gave us a flurried and excited account of the bad treatment his people were subjected to by the white men on board the ship—how they had been struck and even kicked by them, while working at the pumps, and saying that there would be a disturbance if this was not put a stop to. He requested me to accompany him back to the ship, and expostulate with the white men, saying, that if I would explain to them the proper line of conduct to pursue towards the Indians, he would explain to his own people the steps that had been taken on their behalf. This I willingly consented to do, feeling somewhat indignant that the good name of Englishmen should be brought into disrepute by these Yankees, who had borrowed it for their own convenience and security.

On going on board I represented to them the impropriety and, indeed, the impolicy of their conduct, as by thus recklessly causing ill-blood between themselves and the Indians, they ran the risk of drawing down upon themselves the vengeance of the whole tribe. Pe Sha Klim also used his best endeavours to soothe the irritated feelings of his own people, and we left, after having received the assurance of the crew of the "Florentia" that the Indians should be better treated in future. Having thus restored mutual good understanding between the white men and the red skins, I made arrangements for the Indians to supply the former with potatoes, dried salmon, and rock-cod, for which they were to receive payment in tobacco, which, although much damaged by sea-water, was still acceptable.

Having had so much to say about Pe Sha Klim himself, I feel it would be ungallant to take leave of him without some notice of his spouse, who as wife of the spouter, was a person of some importance in the tribe. Mrs. Pe Sha Klim was, undoubtedly, after her peculiar style, a showy dresser, and I should imagine led the fashion among the Mowichat belles. Her wardrobe was extensive and varied, and the really tasteful manner in which the gaily-coloured blankets she wore were ornamented and embroidered, testified to her skill with the needle. Strips of crimson cloth, not inartistically disposed on a ground of blue, and ornamented with an infinite number of small pearl buttons, formed, as may be supposed, a very gorgeous article of apparel. The manner in which she made use of the vermilion paint, so extensively patronized by all Indians, formed a striking contrast to that of other women. She applied it sparingly, and really made it produce the effect of rouge; whereas, all the other women we saw laid it on in a thick bright dab, and the wife of Mocoola himself had not sufficient taste to lead her to apply it in any other fashion.

Before leaving Nootka we notified to Pe Sha Klim that we wished to leave a letter for any man-of-war or other vessel that might put into Friendly Cove. With a view of attracting the attention of any such visitor, we painted the word "Notice" in large letters on the tranverse beam of an Indian hut, suspending the letter itself underneath in a waterproof bag—Pe Sha Klim enjoining on all his followers not to touch it. Our object in doing this was to give information to any vessel that might arrive in search of the "Florentia," where she was to be found. Such a vessel might, in fact, be expected at any moment, as I forgot to mention that a portion of the crew of the "Florentia" had left in an Esquihat canoe for Victoria, the day before we first sighted her, conveying intelligence of her wreck.

One interesting fact in connection with the Indians inhabiting the shores of Nootka Sound I must mention before taking leave of them.

Endeavouring one wet day to elicit all the information we could from them, we found that they preserved a tradition of the visit of white men in a King George's ship many years ago. From the description they gave, very little doubt was left in my mind that it referred to the visit of Captain Cook. They said the ship was in Resolution Cove, and that one of the Indians in getting on board hurt his thigh, the wound being dressed by the surgeon of the ship. An account of this very occurrence will be found in the published narrative of Cook's Voyages.

## CHAPTER IX.

We leave Nootka Sound—Variable Winds—Bajo Reef—We part our Cable—A Favourable Wind—Our Prospects brighten—We fail to make Clayoquot Sound—Our Former Visit—Summer Village of the Clayoquot Indians—Their Warlike Character—Murder of Esquihat Chief—Narrow Escape of a White Man—A Battle in Canoes—Midnight Attack—We re-enter Juan de Fuca Straits—Return to Victoria—Christmas in Vancouver's Island—General Improvements.

WE left Nootka Sound about 3 a.m. The wind failed us abreast of Escalante, a very dangerous reef, extending some distance from the land, and which we had good reason to remember on the occasion of our former visit, having had great difficulty in clearing it on making Nootka Sound. The fresh-sets again carried us some distance out, the wind being intermittent, but the sea heavy. Being afraid of missing our anchorage, we therefore put her round, and ran for Friendly Cove. The wind, up to this point from the south-east, now chopped round and blew directly out of Nootka Sound. We thus beat, all night through, between it and Escalante Reef, the wind always going round to the south-east if we ran out to sea to try for a fair breeze. With daylight we made sure of getting into Friendly Cove, and were, at one time, within two miles of it, but the wind proved very variable and uncertain, never blowing in one quarter long, and as soon as we put our ship about she broke off. The breeze would at intervals die away entirely, until there was not sufficient to keep our sails asleep.

The day was foggy at times, and towards evening we found ourselves drifting to the northward and westward. Late at night it was reported to us that we had been in shoal water for some time; we ordered the lead to be hove, and found from seventeen to nineteen fathoms. This being shallower than we considered we ought to find it, we kept a sharp look-out ahead, and in a short time perceived breakers, in spite of the hazy condition of the atmosphere. We let go our anchor, and were delighted to find that she held. There was no wind, but a big swell. My readers will understand that our night's repose was by no means uninterrupted or undisturbed. We had at once conjectured that we must be close on the Bajo Reef, constant study of the chart having made us thoroughly acquainted with the configuration of the coast, and especially with this most formidable reef.

Daylight found us still, happily, holding to our anchor. The fog, which was dense, slightly clearing away at times, we were enabled to catch a distant sight of the shores of Nootka Sound. These occasional glimpses, affording us a view of two well-known points, enabled us to define our exact position by cross bearings, which verified our original conjecture as to our proximity to Bajo Reef. Symptoms of the wind coming from the westward in light puffs led us to hope that it would eventually go round to this most favourable quarter.

About three in the afternoon, to our great surprise, we found we must be drifting, as the Bajo Reef was evidently receding. We at once hauled in a few fathoms of rope, which soon revealed the fact that we had parted our anchor. We found, when we had hauled it all in, that our cable had been fairly cut in two by friction on the rocks below.

After drifting a very short distance, the breeze sprang up and gradually increased from the westward, and we were devoutly thankful to leave the dreaded Bajo Reef behind, and also to find that we had at length got what we had so long wished for, a fair wind for Victoria. Up to this time we had been apprehensive of having to spend our Christmas at sea, with probably no better fare than unsavoury dried salmon and biscuit, and we could not help smiling when we reflected how differently most of our brother members of the Thames Yacht Club would probably be engaged at that festive season.

From this period, however, we plucked up a new heart of courage; at six we passed the reef at Estevan Point, sixteen miles distant, showing that our vessel *could* travel if she only had a fair chance, and stand well up to her canvas too. What eloquent language did she discourse to our ears as she cleft her way through the bright green waves, and what pleasure was it to feel her as obedient withal to her helm as the most sensitive horse to the slightest motion of the rein, seeming to delight in her escape from the thraldom of adverse winds to which she had been subjected so long!

On first feeling the breeze, we had intended to make Esquihat Harbour and pay a visit to our old acquaintances the Indians of that name there located, but by the time we were off the entrance to the bight, up which their village lies, we found the night had grown much too dark for us to attempt it, and therefore resolved to run on so as to make Clayoquot Harbour with morning. To effect this, finding the wind stand to us, we deemed it expedient to heave our vessel to about midnight, letting her have just enough canvas to hold her own. Although the wind had somewhat increased, and it was now blowing all we could desire, our little craft behaved like a duck. I kept the first watch from eight to twelve myself, and when she was hove to, retired to my bunk, bent on a good night's rest, and feeling more contented with myself and with the world in general than I had done for the last four or five weeks, leaving the vessel in charge of a friend, who had been my companion throughout the cruise, and who had cheerfully shared with me the duties and fatigues incident to a life at sea. He was possessed of that happy temperament that accommodates itself readily to circumstances, and wrapped in a pilot jacket, pipe in mouth, could make himself as happy on deck in a stormy November night, in the Pacific, as in the comfortable smoking-room of his London Club.

On going on deck next morning, I found that we had drifted some seven or eight miles out to sea, nearly abreast of the Point we had to make for. We put her round, and did our best to reach it; the wind and tide, however, proved too much for us. By 10 a.m. we were close in shore, some few miles to the southward, and by 12, after beating during the interval, found ourselves still further to the south. In justice to the sailing qualities of our craft, we must state that she could easily have beat up against wind alone; it was the tremendously powerful tide that proved too much for us.

We spoke a couple of canoes off Clayoquot, and

their crews informed us that there were still some of the white men of the "Florentia" at Esquihat, and that two of them had gone on to Alberni, Barclay Sound, where there is a white settlement.

Finding it impossible to reach our harbour against wind and tide, we at length resolved to make a fair wind of it, and run straight for Victoria. We did not therefore visit Clayoquot on this occasion, but, having been there before, I will for a short time detain my readers, while I, in imagination, take them on shore.

Clayoquot is a very extensive Sound, having several arms or inlets communicating with the interior. The anchorage is generally good, but the water is much shallower, and the shores lower than at Nootka. The growth of timber is less dense, and there is some good open land in its vicinity. The summer village of the Clayoquots is situated near the sea, the entrance to the cove on which it stands being surrounded with rocks and exposed to the most dangerous winds from the sea; in fact, offering no shelter to any vessel seeking refuge there. On proceeding farther up the Sound, however, plenty of places may be found in which a vessel can lie safely at anchor. We were much struck with the immense size of some of the beams of timber used in the construction of several of the huts in this village, those of the chiefs being here, as elsewhere, the largest.

It is indeed astonishing and unaccountable how these savages ever managed to raise a beam near, or quite a hundred feet in length, and from three to four feet in diameter at the larger end, to a height of ten or twelve feet from the ground. The sight of these buildings produced much the same effect of wonder on my mind as did the first visit to Stonehenge. I may mention that many of these erections are evidently of great antiquity.

The Clayoquots are among some of the most warlike tribes on the Island, and their government would appear to differ from that generally met with among Indians. In most cases, as far as we could understand, there would seem to be two chiefs—one hereditary, and another who leads the warriors to battle, and who is probably chosen for his valiant deeds of arms. These functions are united in the chief of the Clayoquots, who is, in fact, a military despot, and the present chief, Seta Kanim, rules in virtue of his prowess in the field.

His reputation as a warrior is very great, and I have heard his deeds of arms referred to by all the Indian tribes inhabiting the entire western coast of Vancouver's Island; at the same time I am bound to confess that among the white men he is not generally well-spoken of, being regarded as unscrupulous and overreaching, as well as insolent and quarrelsome. The influence he exercises over

K

his own people is considered as being adverse to friendly commercial relations between them and the Colonists.

Whatever others may, however, think of this interesting savage, there can be no doubt that in his own estimation Seta Kanim unites in his own dusky, unkempt, and not over savoury individuality the attributes and dignity of an Indian Alexander, Charlemagne, and Haroun-al-Raschid.

As regards my own personal intercourse with the famous chief of the Clayoquots, I remember that the first time he favoured us with a visit on board my yacht, he was very eager that I should examine credentials with which he had been furnished by white men who had visited this part of the island, and to which he evidently attached no small importance. Of course I was happy to comply with his request, but must acknowledge that the result of my scrutiny was, to say the least of it, perplexing, as the testimony produced was of a very contradictory character. For instance, some of the testimonials would be worded somewhat after this fashion:—" This is Seta Kanim, chief of the Clayoquots, he has been on board our vessel, and we have found him honest and trustworthy;" while others set forth his merits in the following style:—" This is Seta Kanim, as great a rascal as is to be met with among the red skins;" or, " This is Seta Kanim, a villain that would murder his own father for a groat, if we may judge from the lying, deceit, and treachery he has practised in his dealings with ourselves." However, we know that where ignorance is bliss the proverb goes on to show the folly of enlightenment, and this certainly was the case with Seta Kanim, who evidently attached the greatest value and importance to these precious documents, and we cannot say that we felt it any business of ours to undeceive him.

Having thus, as he conceived, enhanced his dignity and greatness in our eyes, he no doubt thought it right that we should, in turn, submit our credentials to his inspection, and therefore asked to see my papers. This unexpected demand I at first felt to be somewhat embarrassing, until a bright idea flashing across my mind. I dived below and brought up the diploma of a Royal Arch-Mason, with its showy emblematic device, and its important looking, large red seals. This, with the certificate of a master mason, evidently produced the desired effect, and impressed Seta Kanim with the idea that I really must be a Tyhee of no inconsiderable importance.

The ferocity of these lawless and blood-thirsty savages will be best illustrated by the following incident, which fell under the observation of our interpreter during a former sojourn in this district. He was, at the time we refer to, trading between Victoria and the different Indian villages on this coast, having a small depôt or store in Clayoquot Sound, close to the village. Being, on one occasion, about to start for Victoria, from the village of the Achazats (a tribe which must not be confounded, on account of the similarity of their name, with Achuzats, inhabiting Clayoquot Sound), the sub-chief asked him if he would, as a favour, take him with him to Victoria, as he had never been there, and was very desirous of visiting that place. Having complied with the wish of the sub-chief, and given him a berth on board his schooner, he had occasion, on his way down the coast, to put into Clayoquot Sound, and well knowing that the bitterest animosity existed between the Indians there and the Achazats, he enjoined on his travelling companion not to show himself if he valued his life. Some strange instinct seems however to guide an Indian in tracking and discovering a foe, wherever he may be concealed. They are very bloodhounds in scenting their prey. The unfortunate Achazat chief, although he never showed himself on deck, was nevertheless discovered, and dragged forth by his terrible and remorseless foes. And, in spite of all the efforts made by the white man to prevent it, in spite of his most urgent remonstrances, and even threats, the head of this unhappy Indian was severed from his body before his eyes, the ghastly trophy being afterwards fixed on a pole, in company with the heads of four others of his tribe, who had previously suffered the same fate.

After this tragic occurrence our friend dared not for some time revisit the district inhabited by the Achazats, as they would infallibly have visited the murder of their kinsman on his head—such being the Indian code of justice. After the space of about two years, however—thinking, perhaps, that this desire for vengeance had passed away, or relying on his own tact and talent in managing Indians—he resolved on trusting himself once more among them, notwithstanding that the Clayoquots assured him that it would be courting certain death for him to do so, as the law of blood for blood is irrevocable among all Indians. On arriving in the Sound, on which the village of the Achazats is situated, as soon as the Indians recognized his schooner, they put off in shoals, with blackened faces and arms, and, boarding his little vessel, carried him off a prisoner. According to all the precedents of Indian warfare, his fate would now appear certain, and had he not been a white man, no doubt his head would have been cut off on the spot. Meanwhile, he assumed an air of passive indifference, which, although we can hardly suppose he felt it, yet served, no doubt, to impress the Indians in his favour. While he was lying thus bound in the midst of the village he could hear the chiefs taking counsel among themselves as to what should be his fate. The women, from the first, had pleaded in his favour, and they now urged, fairly enough, that it was through no fault of his that their kinsman was murdered; that, as a white man, he could never have desired the blood of a red skin, and that they had, therefore, no right to take his.

Whether the chiefs dreaded the possible vengeance of the white men if they put one of their number to death, or whether they were induced to listen to reason by the women, certain it is their gentler counsels prevailed, and he was restored to liberty; nor was this all—feeling that, if he were innocent, they must have been guilty of an act of injustice in detaining him a prisoner, they made him a present of several hundred gallons of oil as an indemnification.

He also related to us how, at a subsequent period, he chanced to be spectator of a battle fought in canoes. The Achazats, coming in strength, challenged the Clayoquots to fight them in their harbours. Seta Kanim, nothing loath, forthwith equipped his rude galleys for war, and a veritable naval engagement was the result.

Shortly after the execution of the Achazat chief above referred to, a midnight attack on the Clayoquots was organized by the former tribe to avenge his death. The favourite moment for these murderous night-attacks is a few minutes after midnight, when, according to their theory, sleep is most profound.

Everything being in readiness, they stole noiselessly on the village of their enemies, and each warrior having reached the foot of the couch of his sleeping foeman, with drawn knife in hand, at a pre-concerted signal, and with a deafening war-whoop, the work of slaughter commenced—all arms having been previously secured, and every way of escape cut off. A party of the Clayoquots—scouts—happening, however, to return just at this juncture, a fierce hand-to-hand encounter ensued on the beach, in which many were killed on both sides. But I daresay my readers are tired of the horrors of Indian warfare; we will therefore take leave of the red man and his doings for the present, and make the best of our way back to Victoria.

About midnight on the 6th of December we passed Bonilla Point, and about four in the morning, we once more sighted the light on Cape Classet, the wind still favourable, though hauling a little more off shore. On entering Juan de Fuca Straits, the wind failed us altogether, and a nasty chopping sea delayed our course for some time. In the afternoon, fearing we were losing ground, we ran into ten fathoms water and anchored. A canoe came off and told us, among other things, that there had been two ships wrecked here during the late gales. The tide turning about six, we once more got under weigh, the wind springing up later in the night. It was somewhat disheartening next morning, however, to find that we could still see Bonilla Point, showing we had not made much way during the night. The sea still troublesome, but, a fair wind springing up, we succeeded in making Port St. Juan this day, to the great satisfaction of all on board, as it was only now that we could fairly say our chief difficulties and dangers were over. Up to the moment of making Port St. Juan, we could not feel sure that we might not have to run for Barclay Sound, that being the nearest harbour, in the event of an adverse gale of wind springing up. We saw several canoes of Indians gathering mussels—one came off and offered us some for sale. This was the first time we had been asked for money by an Indian since leaving Nanaimo, October 11.

After being baffled by shifting, uncertain winds and adverse currents, with occasional nasty seas, for a couple of days longer, by which time our provisions were almost gone, and we were reduced to the expedient of boiling our coffee four successive times, to eke out our scanty allowance, and to live almost entirely on Indian dried fish, we at length passed the well-known Race-Rocks, round which the tide was running with its usual velocity. We now caught sight for the first time of the new light at Esquimalt, and finally reached Victoria on the morning of the 12th of December, after an absence of two months and a half.

Our return created quite a sensation in the colony, as at one time considerable doubt and apprehension was felt concerning our fate. On entering the harbour several boats put off to welcome us, and to inquire if we could give any information concerning several wrecks which were supposed to have occurred during our trip.

We must confess we were not sorry to exchange the toils and hardships of our late mode of life for the ease and comforts of civilization. The first few days on shore we spent in looking up our old friends and acquaintances, in whose houses we found preparations everywhere going on to celebrate the forthcoming festivity of Christmas in suitable style. The rooms were decorated with green, and everything was done so much in the fashion of Old England, that we could almost fancy ourselves at home once more, the weather also being sufficiently cold to bear out the illusion.

Christmas in Australia bears no resemblance to an English Christmas, but Christmas in this colony is really wonderfully like its original in the old country, and we can bear ready testimony to the generally hospitable character of the colonists.

We found that the Indians, who, at the time of our arrival in the colony, enjoyed the privilege of encamping where they pleased, had been banished to the other side of the harbour, and on the space formerly occupied by their hovels along the eastern shore, we saw warehouses and other tenements in the course of erection; everything, in fact, gave signs of increasing prosperity. The Indians in the neighbourhood of this town, seem to have learned to respect the authority of the white man, and conform in their intercourse with him to many of the customs of civilization; we have occasionally seen them dressed like Englishmen. Those, however, who have only recently arrived, but who have made a little money by the sale of skins, &c., are very fond of displaying themselves in public in all the gorgeous array of savage finery. I have often been much amused at seeing young Indians of the Hydahs, Bella-Bellas, and other northern tribes—swells of the first water in their own estimation—who will parade the streets of Victoria, two or three abreast, arrayed in embroidered blankets of various colours, a feather fastened by a bright silk handkerchief to their heads, and their faces painted all the colours of the rainbow. The strangest of all sights, however, is perhaps that of an Indian woman in crinoline, which may also not unfrequently be witnessed here.

## CHAPTER X.

We revisit British Columbia—The Fraser River and Gold-Fields—New Westminster—The Harrison Lilooett Route described—Skaholet Indians—Harrison River and Lake—Port Douglas—Encampment of Royal Engineers—Strong Current—Chinese Gold-Seekers—Fort Hope—Romantic Scenery—Tum Sioux Indians—Religious Ceremony—" Tumanas," or " Medicine Man "—Route from Fort Hope to Lilooett, on the way to Cariboo.

I WILL now once more ask the reader to accompany us to the mainland, while I describe the different routes leading to the world-famous gold regions of British Columbia. The Fraser River—which drains the waters of the auriferous districts—has its source in the Rocky Mountains, and is composed of two main streams, both of which are gold producing. The southern branch of the Fraser, rising in these mountains, after a course of near three hundred miles, receives its northern tributary, which is fed by a chain of lakes at Fort George, from which point the junction of the two forms the Fraser River proper. I may here pause to remark that the whole of the tributaries of the Fraser flowing from the east, that is to say, those which have their source in the Rocky Mountains, are found to be auriferous, while those from the west are, generally speaking, not so. This would seem to indicate that these mountains are the true source of all the gold met with as deposits in the bed and banks of these streams, a theory which is, moreover, supported by the fact that gold is also found on the opposite or eastern slope of the Rocky Mountains —as, for instance, in the Saskatchewan and other streams.

It must not be supposed, however, that even the vast extent of territory drained by the Fraser and its tributaries comprises the whole of the gold producing portion of British Columbia, which probably extends completely across the country from its southern to its northern boundary. At the entrance to the Fraser River we meet with a sand-bank or bar, which—although not presenting any serious obstacle to navigation—is, nevertheless, troublesome, as the channel through it is narrow, and the depth of water never very great. The country near the mouth is low and swampy, overgrown with reeds, and producing a quantity of coarse grass, which is, however, both here and at Langley converted into hay.

The Fraser is not navigable for sea-going vessels far above New Westminster, the capital, which therefore discharge their cargoes generally into the flat-bottomed steamers, worked by a single wheel in the stern, which are employed in the navigation of the river above this point.

On passing Fort Langley the river narrows and becomes still shallower, but continues navigable for the steamers I have spoken of, as far as Fort Hope and Yale. Here the mountains close in upon the river, forming a gorge through which it flows in places with great impetuosity, and further navigation becomes impossible. We have now, however, reached the auriferous portion of its course.

New Westminster, the capital of British Columbia, is situated, as I have already mentioned, in a clearing on the right bank of the river. The growth of timber is here very dense, but the process of clearing the land in its neighbourhood is rapidly going on, and the sharp ring of the backwoodsman's axe is continually heard; while, ever and anon, the sound of crashing boughs proclaims that one of the giants of the forest has yielded to the vigour and dexterity with which this hardy race of men ply their toilsome vocation. The most difficult and troublesome portion of their work remains, however, to be done, after the tree is felled, where it is necessary to clear the ground, and consists in grubbing up the stump and roots of the tree, or more generally destroying them by fire, or blasting.

Some distance above Langley the Fraser receives the waters of the Harrison River, whose bright, clear blue stream contrasts with the muddy waters of the former. We have now reached the point at which the two principal routes to the diggings diverge, the one lying up the Harrison, through Port Douglas, and by a chain of lakes and road to Cayoshe.

On leaving Port Douglas, at the head of Harrison Lake, the route lies through a wild and mountainous district of an eminently picturesque character. This portion of the journey we performed on mules, but since then stage coaches have been substituted for these animals. The scenery here is quite Alpine in its character, the road being frequently at a dizzy height above the Harrison River, which flows foaming and roaring far beneath. This road was in process of formation by the Royal Engineers, at the period of our visit to their encampment near Port Douglas, to which I shall hereafter allude.

A distance of about twenty-nine miles now brings us to Lake Lilooett, from which a road, about sixteen miles in length—along which it was proposed to lay a tramway—brings us to Lake Anderson, closely followed by Lake Seaton; having traversed which, a stretch of road once more lies before us, at the extremity of which is Cayoshe or Lilooett, whence to Fort Alexander, in the midst of the gold country and on the confines of the Cariboo district, the route is comparatively easy. This route to the gold regions of British Columbia is generally spoken of now as the Harrison Lilooett route. I may mention that the whole of these lakes are traversed by steamers, with the exception of a very small one which I have not specified, and which is crossed in an open boat. The scenery throughout is romantically beautiful, and the trip in fine weather is a very pleasant one, barring mosquitoes.

At the mouth of the Harrison River a tribe of Indians known as the Skaholets are located. The huts composing their village are more than usually distinguished for the amount of curious and elaborate carving they display, evidently of great antiquity. These Indians make a great profession of their adherence to the Roman Catholic faith. They have a strong objection to perform any kind of labour on a Sunday, and many of them exhibited papers they had received from Roman Catholic missionaries, stating that they were ".temperance men," and begging that no white man would, by the offer of any kind of intoxicating drink, tempt them to depart from their self-imposed abstinence. I have occasionally seen these Indians fishing in the Harrison, suspended in a rude sort of cradle attached to the projecting bough or stem of a tree, overhanging the roaring waters of this impetuous stream as it rushed between its rocky and precipitous banks—a picturesque, but it appeared to me dangerous mode of angling, as had the fisherman been precipitated by any accident into the torrent beneath, I think his chances of escape would have been small indeed. He did not appear himself, however, to be troubled by any apprehensions of the sort, but pursued his employment as unconcernedly as if in a place of perfect safety.

In ascending the Harrison I found the scenery very picturesque. The river was now narrowed to a mountain torrent in some rocky gorge, now spread into a charming lake in the open country, the water itself being of the most beautiful ultramarine blue. The general character of the scenery on these small lakes is thought by some travellers greatly to resemble certain districts in the Highlands of Scotland, and may fairly vie with the noble scenery in the vicinity of Fort Hope on the Fraser River. Port Douglas, some eight or ten miles from the mouth, is situated on the Harrison Lake, and a very beautiful and romantic little lake it appeared to me the first time I beheld it, its intensely blue waters rippled by a fresh breeze and flecked with the white foam of its mimic billows, the various little islands scattered over its surface, and the surrounding panorama of mountain and rock, on which the mingled foliage of a variety of forest trees relieved the sombre hues of the pine, combined to form a picture of no ordinary beauty and freshness. At the same time I must confess that, beautiful as it is, we must beware how we trust, ourselves at all times on its treacherous surface, as the lake is subject to sudden and violent squalls very dangerous to the smaller kinds of sailing vessels. Its waters are also much encumbered with floating timber, which, both here and on the Fraser River, is a frequent source of injury to the steamers. These vessels, consequently, always carry with them the means of repairing any injury that may befall them on the spot; the snags in the Fraser River are especially dangerous. These steamers are all of the type of the American river-boat, and are, as a matter of necessity, provided with very powerful engines to enable them to stem the rapid current. They all work by high pressure. The way in which any canoes we chanced to meet shot past us as we were ascending this stream, was quite sufficient to give us an idea of its force and rapidity.

Fort Douglas, at the head of Harrison Lake, consists of two or three stores, a church, several whisky shops, and a Customs office. In summer it is hardly habitable on account of mosquitoes, the plague of British Columbia. These troublesome insects are found to be diminishing in proportion to the amount of timber felled. The general appearance of Fort Douglas, situated as it is in a wild mountainous district, quite Alpine in its character, forcibly recalled some of the little Swiss or Tyrolese villages one meets with among the Alps.

I rode out from Douglas to visit some friends, at the camp of the Royal Engineers, who were engaged here in making a road to open a communication with the interior. The road, as far as it was then finished, lay through a wild, rocky district; on the left hand of it flowed the Harrison, sometimes broad and shallow, brawling over stones, sometimes deep and narrow, and rushing through a gorge. My friends at the camp gave me a hearty welcome, entertaining me in a style of rough hospitality, such as was alone compatible with surrounding circumstances. Rum or whisky, mingled with the water of the river, was set before us on a rude deal table, under a shed of new pine planks, which was both thatched and carpeted with fresh pine branches; those above being placed to keep off the too ardent rays of the sun, while those under foot both served as a carpet and filled the air with a pungent aromatic fragrance when trodden on. We spent some hours very pleasantly discussing old scenes, old friends, and old adventures, and I did not start until after nightfall on my ride back, which was consequently of a very wild and solitary character.

We will now retrace our steps, and ascend the

Fraser River to Fort Hope. The current in this part of its course is tremendous, and the difficulty of stemming it proportionately great. The steamers seldom succeed in achieving a higher speed than from one to two knots per hour, and I have known them not to make an inch for hours together. On the occasion of the trip I am now describing, our steamer made fast a rope to the trunk of a tree, to assist in stemming the current. This broke, however, but some of our party happening to be on shore, were lucky enough to catch the broken end, and make it fast to another tree. I, in company with several others, performed the remainder of the distance to Fort Hope on foot, leaving the steamer to battle with the current as best she could. We passed several parties of Chinamen, washing the sands of the river for gold, the rockers being generally worked by parties of from three to four. The number of Chinese to be met with all over the world, wherever gold has been discovered, is a singular and characteristic fact. They are to be found in Australia, California, and now here, and in great numbers. Being frugal, persevering, and abstemious, they generally succeed, not only in purchasing their enfranchisement of the agent who has shipped them from their own country and supplied them with the few necessaries they required on arriving, but also in taking back with them a competence on their return home. One whole street in Victoria is filled with them—it is called Pandora Street; walking through it, one might almost fancy oneself in Canton. This is also the head-quarters of the merchants, who have their stores here, and many of whom do a very considerable trade.

On reaching Fort Hope we got some Indians to ferry us across in a canoe, we being on the right bank of the river, while the Fort is situated on the left bank. Having effected the passage with some difficulty, the current being still very strong, we landed in the little town which has recently grown up around the original Hudson's Bay Fort. The old fort, which I remembered in its primitive state, has been done away with, and the town, as it now stands, consists of two or three streets, and a few stores or shops. Soon after landing, the shrill whistle of the steamer coming up showed she was not far behind us.

Fort Hope is situated at an angle or bend of the Fraser River, and at its junction with the Coquiklum. The latter is a very picturesque little mountain stream, the waters of which being fed by melting snows, are intensely cold, and are said to abound in excellent trout.

Fort Hope occupies the centre of a panorama of mountain scenery, of the most grand and beautiful description, forming a fitting prelude to the wild and terrible character of that to be met with above

Yale, where the Fraser River flows between two almost perpendicular walls of naked rocks of dizzy height.

Adjoining Fort Hope is the village of the Tum Sioux Indians. It presents the usual characteristics of an Indian village, but we must not omit to mention that, in addition to these their ordinary habitations, this tribe have a number of holes dug in the earth, which, when roofed over, are intended to form their dwelling-places in very severe weather.

On the occasion of one of my visits to this village, I heard sounds of chanting, in which many voices were mingled, issuing from one of the larger huts, and bearing a striking resemblance in their general character to a Roman Catholic service. My curiosity being aroused, I essayed to enter, but was arrested on the threshold by a functionary in a blanket, who evidently filled the office of a Tum Sioux "Bumble." After a time, however, I was admitted, and before the service was entirely concluded. I found a party of Indians, to the number of thirty or forty, engaged in bowing and crossing themselves in the intervals of chanting. I did not observe that they made use of any of the emblems of the Romish Church, but feel sure that the atmosphere of the place in which they were assembled would, at any rate, have been greatly improved by the introduction of a little incense.

I doubt whether these poor savages attached any particular meaning or significance to any of the rites and ceremonies in the performance of which they were engaged. They had, no doubt, been told by the Roman Catholic missionaries, who had been their instructors, that it was klosh (good) for them to act after this fashion, and therefore did their best in their rude way to carry out the injunctions of their teachers.

Before taking leave of our Indian friends, of whom I hope the reader is not yet wearied, I must say a few words about that important functionary the "Tumanas," as he is called on the western shores of Vancouver, or Medicine Man. His post is, I believe, a lucrative one, but at the same time, as a set off against its advantages, should a patient happen to expire under his treatment—a consummation by no means improbable, considering the nature of the curative process—it is quite within the limits of possibility that the friends and relatives of the deceased may take it into their heads to sacrifice the unfortunate "Tumanas" to the manes of their relatives.

The mode of treatment adopted by the "Medicine Man" consists generally in creating a frightful uproar in the chamber of the sick person, whether with the design of arousing the drooping faculties of the patient or of scaring away evil spirits, I never could rightly ascertain, but know that I have often felt the greatest commiseration for the unfortunate sick who have to undergo the suffering of such an ordeal, at a time when quiet and repose are more than ever desirable. I have seen the unhappy victims of perhaps a bilious attack, accompanied by violent headache, or the weakened and debilitated sufferers from recent fever, tortured by the insensate method of cure adopted by the Tumanas, who persists in dancing about the apartment and yelling at the top of his voice, and, as if this were not noise enough, accompanying himself meanwhile by the horrid uproar of a couple of Indian rattles, one in either hand. When I inform the reader that the latter instruments consist of two hollow pieces of wood, bound together by cords, and filled with loose stones, he will be able to realize at once the delectable sounds they may be made to produce, and the very great probability of their being conducive to the comfort of a sick-room. To crown all, the Medicine Man will occasionally vary his performances by administering smart blows to the patient in various parts of his body—in plain English, boxing his ears and thumping his chest.

I remember that on one of the first occasions of my witnessing the extraordinary performances of the Tumanas, they appeared to me so extremely ludicrous that, in spite of my utmost efforts, I could not forbear laughing outright. One of the relatives of the sick person, who was looking on in a state of silence and composure, probably not unmixed with awe, bent on me from time to time looks of reproving gravity, until at length, finding that these failed to check my irresistible inclination to laugh, he abruptly exclaimed, with mingled indignation and astonishment, "Kopa kha mika hee hee?"—"What are you laughing at?"

The journey from Fort Hope to Yale is performed by steamer, at which point we reach the limit of navigation on the Fraser River. Above this, it is practicable, occasionally, only for canoes. The remainder of the route from Yale to Lillooett, by way of Lytton, is performed by means of horses or mules, or on foot. We have now once more reached the starting point for the gold fields to which I had already conducted our readers, by the Harrison Lillooett route. I may mention that a waggon road has been completed, which opens a communication between Fort Hope and the Similkameen country, a district lying to the east of Fort Hope, and to the south of Cariboo, and the gold fields of the Fraser River.

## CHAPTER XI.

General Remarks on British Columbia—Its Soil and Climate—Agricultural Prospects—Its Natural Productions—Mineral, Vegetable, and Animal—Suitability of its Climate to rearing English Stock—Encouragement to Farmers to settle here—The Gold Fields—Prospects of Miners—Advice to Gold Seekers—A Miner's Narrative—Different Methods of seeking for Gold—Other Branches of Industry—Packers—Effect of the Discovery of Gold on British Columbia—Geographical Features of the Country—Its Mountains, Rivers, and Lakes.

THE rapid growth into important and flourishing colonies of wild and inhospitable regions on the distant sea-board of the Pacific, is among those phenomena of our age, which, from time to time, arise to startle us into the belief that the world really does move faster than of yore. Casting our eyes in whatsoever direction we may, we cannot fail to realize the fact that events are daily passing around us which must be fraught with the deepest interest to the future history of our race. The recent impetus which has been given to those colonies which it is our province specially to consider, is, no doubt, due to the artificial stimulus imparted by the discovery of gold. Now this, though useful as an adjunct, is not sufficient in itself even to create a new colony, much less ensure its future prosperity. Gold cannot effect impossibilities, it cannot clothe the surface of the naked rock, or the sandy desert with verdure; nor can it develope a prosperous commercial community in a region destitute of natural harbours and rivers.

It behoves us therefore to consider whether, independently of the accident of their mineral wealth, they possess within themselves the essential elements of true prosperity. This is a question which we think can be satisfactorily answered in the affirmative, and we believe that these colonies will be found to present as attractive a field for emigration to the farmer and capitalist, as to the gold-digger, the artisan, and the labourer.

In the interior of British Columbia are vast tracts of great fertility, capable of conversion into the finest agricultural and pastoral lands. The supply of the mining districts, and the different towns and settlements in their vicinity, with fresh meat and vegetables, will, no doubt, for the present, engage the attention of the stock-keepers and agriculturist, and prove a lucrative speculation; we hope it may ultimately be the means of introducing farming on an extensive scale into this country. I would strongly recommend any who have the means of doing so, and are inclined to turn their attention to this branch of industry, to take stock into the interior, where the rearing of cattle, sheep, and pigs cannot fail amply to indemnify them for their trouble and outlay. With regard to the last-mentioned animals, it may be observed that the Chinese—of which race there are so many to be found in the gold districts—scarcely ever eat any other kind of meat than pork. There are extensive open districts in the interior of the finest grazing land imaginable, capable of supporting innumerable herds of cattle and flocks of sheep, lying contiguous to the recently constructed high roads and inland water communication, to which I have already drawn the reader's attention. The mules and pack-horses traversing these districts find amply sufficient grazing wherever they are turned out, so as to be entirely independent of any other kind of provender.

The climate is remarkably healthy and bracing, and the air pure. As we advance into the interior, we shall find the cold, during winter, increase in intensity; at the same time the climate is less moist, and less subject to sudden and frequent changes than on the coast.* This being

* Since writing the above, accounts have reached us of the very severe character of the past winter in British Columbia. The

the case, it will naturally be inferred that, with a corresponding excellence of soil, any of the ordinary household vegetables grown in England may also be raised here. That this is the actual fact I can testify from personal experience, having eaten turnips, carrots, potatoes, greens, and other vegetables in British Columbia of a size and quality that would entitle them to admiration anywhere. Of its suitability for the production of our English cereal crops, I cannot speak so positively, as but very small quantities of grain have as yet been raised here; at the same time I think that we are fully

Fraser River was frozen throughout a great portion of its course, with the exception of a few rapids—the journey from Yale to New Westminster having been performed on foot on the ice. The quantity of snow that had fallen was everywhere very great, reaching to the tops of the houses in Yale. A thermometer at the Forks of Quesnelle, Cariboo country, stood at 18° below zero, and at Beaver Lake, on the following day, at 25° below zero. A winter of this degree of severity is, however, quite exceptional. The *Victoria British Colonist*, commenting on this fact, draws the following distinction between the past season and the present:—"From the 1st of February to the 1st of March, 1861, 635 passengers left this port on steamers for British Columbia. Fraser River was opened from Alexandria to its mouth, and miners commenced work on the North Fork of the Quesnelle on the 22nd of February. The trails from Lytton and Cayoosh were in tolerable travelling order during the same period, and scores of miners and animals were wending their way towards the golden land. This year the Fraser, from source to mouth, is blockaded with ice; hardly fifty miners have left this place for British Columbia, and from late and reliable accounts received of the weather and the state of the roads, it would seem to be as much as a man's life were worth to attempt the journey to Quesnelle from either Lytton or Cayoosh before the 1st of June."

justified, from its known qualities of soil and climate, in assuming that abundant and excellent crops of every species of British cereal will eventually be grown in British Columbia.

The vegetable productions indigenous to these regions are wholly unimportant, with the exception, perhaps, of cranberries and wild hemp. Of course, this statement does not include the vast forests of pine and other timber, with which so large a portion of the surface of the country is covered, and which must, for ages to come, form an important article of export. The oak here met with is of stunted growth, and its timber is inferior. Maple-wood, so valuable in cabinet-making, is found in some places, together with cypress, juniper, yew, birch, and poplar.

Of the mineral productions of British Columbia, it is difficult as yet to speak with perfect confidence, save as regards the now world-notorious fact of its auriferous wealth. Both silver and copper are known to exist in considerable quantities, and mines of both metals have recently been opened. I have frequently seen specimens of silver ore brought by Indians to Victoria, from districts lying adjacent to the sea coast.

Coal is known to exist in various districts of British Columbia, but in small quantities only. Stone, suitable for every purpose of building, only requires to be quarried. Limestone and sandstone are everywhere abundant. Marble, of various kinds, is found in the coast range of mountains. Salt exists in many localities, and is obtained in great quantities from the salt springs of Nanaimo, Vancouver's Island. I have already alluded to the coal mines at the latter place, the only spot where coal is at present worked in these colonies. Those interested in the matter have now an opportunity of forming an opinion of the quality of the Nanaimo coal, as a specimen may be inspected at the Great Exhibition.

In enumerating the other principal natural sources of wealth in British Columbia, I must not forget to mention the different species of fur-bearing animals which are met with in abundance along these coasts, as well as those of Vancouver's Island. Indeed, as I have already mentioned, it was in pursuit of furs that the attention of the white man first came to be directed to these wild and inhospitable regions, as they were at one time considered, and the forts of the Hudson's Bay Company have formed the nuclei of some of the principal towns in these colonies.

Among the principal fur-bearing animals found here are the bear, the marten, the mink, the silver fox, the racoon, the otter, the beaver and the seal. The ermine is only met with further north. The sportsman may be interested to know that wild sheep are found in the mountains, but are very difficult to approach. He will, however, have a glorious quarry in the noble elk. This is an entirely different animal from the stag we have already alluded to on Vancouver's Island, and which is also found here. The head of the elk is adorned with noble antlers, frequently weighing upwards of thirty pounds, and its flesh is excellent eating. Notwithstanding the spread of its branching antlers, the elk will make its way through the thickest woods more swiftly than a man can follow; in so doing, it will fling back its stately head till its horns lie level with its back, and bound through the crashing underwood with wonderful speed. These animals are frequently tracked on the snow.

There are two kinds of bear in British Columbia —the black bear, and the grizzly or brown bear. Among the more destructive and troublesome of the other wild animals, may be enumerated the wolf and the puma. The latter is an animal of the cat kind, of a light brown colour, turning to a whitish grey underneath. It varies in size, some of the larger among them attaining to the size of a Newfoundland dog. The puma is a cowardly animal, but very destructive to sheep. I must not forget, finally, to mention that in British Columbia we find the dreaded rattlesnake of the American continent. This formidable reptile is much more plentiful in some districts than in others.

Among the feathered tribes indigenous to this

colony, are the white swan—which is very difficult shooting—several kinds of geese, and a great variety of ducks. Sea-birds are plentiful on the coast. In addition to these, the heron, the blue grouse, and the willow grouse and the snipe are found in the interior. Vast flocks of wild pigeons are occasionally seen; and, finally, among the birds of prey, we may enumerate the eagle, the hawk, and the kite.

I have already alluded to the different kinds of fish taken in the waters of British Columbia and Vancouver, both fresh and salt. These comprise several known varieties of excellent quality, such as rock-cod, herrings, skate, flounders, and river trout. The most important is, undoubtedly, the salmon, which—both fresh and preserved—is excellent eating, and is everywhere very abundant.

Every kind of stock that has been introduced from our own country into British Columbia, has been found to flourish equally well. Sheep, cattle, pigs, and poultry, all seem to thrive and increase. The native horses are small but serviceable. The American cattle in California are fine animals. The Spanish breed, which are numerous, are smaller, but are at the same time valuable stock.

On one very important point we can set at rest any misgivings that may be felt by the farmer who settles in British Columbia. Independently of the protection afforded by the law, we can assure him that he need not feel the least apprehension of successful competition in any other quarter. In spite of the abundance of agricultural produce, and its consequent cheapness in the markets of California and Oregon, the distance it will have to be brought will effectually protect the farmer in British Columbia. If sent from California, it will have to traverse a distance of from one thousand to one thousand five hundred miles; if from Oregon, five hundred to eight hundred; if from Vancouver's Island, one hundred and fifty to five hundred. In every case the expense of transport is so great that nothing but the entire absence of agriculture in central and northern British Columbia, allows a single ounce of Californian or Oregon produce to reach the mines, and is in itself a better protection to agricultural industry than the protective tariff of ten per cent. levied at New Westminster. The moment that domestic produce is raised in sufficient quantities to supply the demand, the importation of foreign produce will that moment cease.

It is impossible to estimate the loss that British Columbia sustained last season, in consequence of her want of agricultural industry. It has been computed at upwards of half a million of dollars. Here is, in itself, a sum that would provide five hundred farmers with an annual profit of one thousand dollars, certainly greater than the average gains realized by diggers. Thus, we see we have a source of wealth capable of yielding higher profits than the gold fields, lying absolutely fallow. What a stimulus ought this reflection to impart to agricultural enterprise and industry! The prospect is equally encouraging to farmers of every description, small as well as great; all may do equally well. For the benefit of those who may be curious to know what prospects the markets at present afford, I will quote the following current prices of produce at the mines. Vegetables can be supplied, at a point distant about eighty miles from the Forks of Quesnelle, at 8 cents per lb.; hay, at 10 cents; barley and oats, at 30 cents. If carried to the mines in the Cariboo country, a distance of from eighty to one hundred miles, vegetables will realize 25 cents per lb.; barley and oats, 50 cents; butter, 1 dollar 50 cents; bacon, 75 cents. I think these are facts that need no comment.

Of course the gold fields must be expected, for some time to come, to form the real attraction for the great mass of immigrants to British Columbia. No doubt a great proportion of these will come from California and Australia; at the same time, if we may judge by the advertisements in the papers of ships to sail for these colonies, thousands must be flocking thither from this country also. I fully expect to hear that there has been a rush to the diggings this summer, and that provisions of all descriptions are at very high prices; and am therefore further prepared to hear that there has been a certain amount of privation and suffering. At the same time I have no doubt that the packers—a class to which I shall have occasion again to allude—will do their best to meet the demand, however great, by an adequate supply of the necessaries of life; their vocation being, as may be supposed, a very lucrative one. With every desire to see the mineral wealth and material resources of British Columbia developed to their fullest extent, I think it right to forewarn the intending digger of certain difficulties and disappointments he may possibly meet with, if he has had no previous experience of this kind of labour. In the first place the gold fields here, as elsewhere, are a lottery, in which, however rich the auriferous deposits, there must, I fear, always be more blanks than prizes. In the second place the life of a digger is one of considerable hardship and privation, such as could be scarcely endured by those accustomed to a sedentary and easy life, and have never known what it is to rough it, as it is expressively termed. They must bear in mind that their only shelter will be a hut of their own construction, or a tent; that beans and bacon, with the addition of plain water as a beverage, are a luxury not always to be commanded. I would recommend all diggers in the enjoyment of good health, religiously to abstain from purchasing the spirits retailed at the "Whisky Stores," as they are termed. These are all of the very vilest description, partaking more or less of the character of the stuff called by the Americans "Tangleleg." Abominable as are these drinks, the price charged for them is nevertheless exorbitant; and there can be no doubt that a whisky store at the diggings generally proves a very lucrative speculation to those that are unscrupulous enough to embark in it. The unfortunate digger, therefore, who takes to drinking, not only parts with a large proportion of the hardly-earned results of his labour, but is, at the same time, undermining his constitution, and rendering himself more and more unfit for future exertions. I have seen and heard of so many instances of the pernicious—the ruinous effect of drink at the diggings, that I cannot refrain from insisting thus strongly on the necessity of total abstinence. Gambling is another vice the gold-digger should scrupulously avoid. I have known cases in which diggers, after parting with the whole of their stock of gold, were mad enough, in the excitement of the moment, to stake their claim, and having lost it, and with it the means of further gain, were reduced to hire themselves out as day-labourers to others.

The intending gold-digger should, in the next place, bear in mind that genuine digging for gold is very hard work; is, in fact, the work of a navvy, and requires the exercise of a very considerable amount of physical strength and endurance.

Gold-finding in British Columbia has hitherto been confined, in the first instance, to washing for gold on the rivers, and latterly to surface-digging. The real hard work of digging, sinking shafts, and tunnelling, such as we hear of in Australia, has yet to come. The cradle or rockers I have seen in use on the rivers consist of a couple of sieves, of different degrees of fineness, fixed one above another; the particles of gold, being separated by degrees from the larger sort of grit and pebbles, fall through, by reason of their weight, and finally adhere to the woolly surface of a blanket disposed to receive them, out of which they are afterwards picked.

For the benefit of those who feel specially interested in the subject of gold digging, we append the following characteristic account of the adventures of a miner, as related by himself in a letter to a friend. The party alluded to started from Yale, above Fort Hope, on the Fraser River:—

"My first trip up the rapids nearly cost me my life. Six of us started in company. We had the usual outfit, a canoe loaded with provisions, mining tools, and haversacks. Four men travelled on shore, and pulled the boat up the stream by a rope attached to its bow; another man and I were in the boat. Suddenly we ran into an eddy, the boat was at once upset, all our traps tumbled into the water, and we were nearly drowned. Luckily we managed to cling to the boat, and were dragged ashore. The loss of my haversack, with all my papers, I regret very much, as I cannot replace them again. We kindled a fire and dried ourselves, then returned to Fort Yale, bought another outfit, started again, and reached the Upper Fraser without any other mishap. Our life on the journey was rough enough. We slept at night round a fire kindled on the bank, ate a half-cooked breakfast before we started in the morning, and then trudged along our weary road. The land on either side of the river for almost the whole distance, is rough and rocky. The tops of the hills are covered with snow all the summer; the wood growing on the sides is shrubby and dwarfed. In some places these hills are bald and peaky, where, apparently, man never trod. Farming is out of the question in these parts. We prospected a short time on some of the bars on our way up, but with very poor success. These bars lie like steps or terraces along the river, the first a few feet above high water mark, from one to three hundred feet —then a level. Sometimes for four or five steps high they are covered with soft sand, from two to ten feet deep, then a layer of gravel from six inches to three feet deep. Below these the gold is deposited, so you see we have a great deal of trouble to remove them before we can reach it.

"On reaching the head of the Lower Fraser, we hired three Indians to assist us in carrying our provisions, and instructed them to conduct us to Swift River. On arriving there we sent back the Indians, and began prospecting up the river. We were three weeks before we found anything. At last we hit upon a spot which paid twenty-five dollars per day each. We were the first white men on that part of the river. An accident occurred here, by which one of our party (a Frenchman) lost his life. When we were moving our camp, he was lifting his gun from behind a stump, when the trigger caught some of the branches and exploded, the charge entering his arm and shoulder, wounding him severely. We doctored him as best we could, but it was of no avail; he died in a few days. We buried him in this wild region, and put a stone over his grave to mark the spot. We wrought along here till our stores were done, and did well. We came down and got another supply of provisions, and on returning we found our diggings covered with Chinamen, who, it seems, had come shortly after we left, and had then nearly worked out. We shouldered our burdens and travelled for eight days further up the river, when we found another piece of ground, which yielded from twenty-five dollars to a hundred dollars per day.

These diggings lasted till the middle of October; by this time we had a considerable amount of gold. The life is hard enough at the diggings. Our bed was of hemlock brush, but the weary miner sleeps sounder on it than many in more comfortable circumstances. With trifling exceptions, such is the life of the miner in all new gold countries."

We must, in conclusion, remember that gold-digging is only practicable in British Columbia during a certain portion of the year, the districts in which the mines are situated being covered many feet deep in snow during the winter months.

That many who leave this country in the sanguine hope of realizing a rapid fortune in the new "El-Dorado" of the West will be disappointed, there can be no doubt; at the same time there are many other ways besides gold-digging of earning a livelihood in new and thriving colonies, like British Columbia and Vancouver's Island, if the emigrant be only willing to work and prepared to turn his hand to anything in which he can be useful. Really skilled artisans may command a very high rate of wages. I have myself paid a carpenter as much as five dollars a day.

The so-called packers are a class employed in supplying the gold-fields with the different necessaries of life; food, clothing, mining-tools, and other indispensable articles being packed in the smallest possible compass on the backs of horses or mules, and disposed of in quarters where they are sure to meet with a ready sale, at prices realizing an immense per-centage.

It will be seen from the general tenor of my foregoing remarks, that I look upon British Columbia as possessing, independently of her gold-fields, no inconsiderable share of the essential elements of success and future prosperity. Of course the discovery of gold is an incalculable boon to a country already possessing so many advantages of soil and climate, and will give an impulse to its material progress in which months will see the work of years accomplished. In directing a tide of immigration to its shores, it will be the means of supplying it with the very element of prosperity of which it stands most in need—strong hands to till its soil and develop those material resources which must ever constitute the true wealth of a country. The prosperity of a new colony like British Columbia is to be guaged by its agricultural produce. If it be not self-supporting, its gold, however abundant, must go to purchase provisions for the hungry mouths of its population, and thus enrich other lands rather than itself; nor do I doubt that, in the main, agricultural pursuits will prove a surer road to wealth than even gold-digging. There can be no doubt, however, that the latter pursuit, in the very uncertainty of its results, exercises over men's minds much of the fascination of the gambling-table, and, of course, the great mass of immigrants, animated by the accounts of the really fabulous sums that were in many cases realized by gold-diggers last season, will rush at once to the gold-fields. In my opinion the wisest and safest plan for those who intend to become gold-seekers would be, where it is practicable, to unite in parties eight or ten strong, on the principle of mutual benefit. Such a party could hardly fail to realize something at the end of the season, as the non-success of some would be compensated for by the gains of others. They would be strong to resist aggression, and in the case of sickness any member would be sure to be carefully tended. I am happy to say that a much greater respect for law and order seems to exist among the gold-diggers of British Columbia than has hitherto characterized this class in other parts of the world, even in our own colonies. No doubt by this time a very considerable sprinkling of Californian rowdies will have been attracted hither; but I hope that the influence of the general good conduct of the mass will be found sufficient to enforce in them a respect for the great principles of order and honesty.

The history of British Columbia for the last few years is a proof of the difficulty of foreseeing the future of a new and, comparatively speaking, unknown region such as this; it also shows how little reliance can be placed in the judgment of those who may be supposed to have the best opportunity of forming a correct opinion. After the settlement of the long-disputed question of boundary between the British Government and the United States, known as the Oregon Question, it was generally supposed that we had been overreached by the " 'cute Yankee," who had taken care to reserve for himself all that was worth having, leaving us a barren and useless tract of swamp, mountain, and forest. How signally have recent events proved the fallacy of such conclusions! Here we find, not only one of the richest—if not the very richest—auriferous region that has yet been discovered, but a country possessing a climate and soil that leave little or nothing to be desired, and abounding in natural advantages that only require to be developed to minister to all the wants and comforts of mankind. In a region equalling France in extent, we shall be prepared to find considerable difference of soil and climate,—the mountain districts being the most barren as well as the coldest in winter.

The whole of British Columbia lies between the Rocky Mountains and the Pacific, and, consequently, on the western water-shed of the great

North American Continent. It is traversed throughout its entire length, from the Simpson's River to its southern boundary, by several chains of mountains, running in a direction from the north-west to the south-east, more or less parallel to the Rocky Mountains, and following, to some extent, the coast-line which the range of mountains known as the "Coast Range" approach more closely in the southernmost part of their course; these, together with the Cascade and other ranges, are prolonged into the Oregon territory.

These mountain ranges form a very picturesque object in the distance, as seen from the sea in sailing from Victoria to Fraser River or any other point on the coast of British Columbia. Several of the peaks attain to a very considerable altitude, being covered with snow in summer. Mount Baker in the south is upwards of 10,000 feet in height.

It is through a gorge in these mountains, above Fort Hope, to which I have already alluded, that the principal river of British Columbia—the Fraser—finds its way to the sea. The scenery of these mountain districts wherever I have traversed them —whether on the Harrison River or on the Fraser above Fort Hope—is of the most romantic and picturesque character, in some parts resembling the Highlands of Scotland, while in others I could fancy myself in Switzerland, the lofty and snow-covered mountains being quite Alpine in their character, and the train of mules carrying baggage through their rugged passes assisting to complete the illusion. Beyond these, at a considerable distance, and also nearly parallel to the Rocky Mountains, is another range of mountains, forming the water-shed of the Fraser and Thompson Rivers on the west, and of the Columbia River on the east.

The coast is indented with a number of creeks or inlets, many of them penetrating far into the interior. Islands are also thickly scattered along the coast—many of them lying between British Columbia and Vancouver's Island—the largest of which is Queen Charlotte's Island, in the Pacific. This has recently been discovered to consist of two larger islands, Graham and Moresby, and one small one, Prevost. This group of islands is the habitat of the Hydah Indians, to whom we have so often alluded, and the principal channel which divides them takes its name of "Skittegat" from the chief of this Indian tribe.

The gold regions of British Columbia lie between these ranges of mountains and the great central chain of the North American continent, the Rocky Mountains. In the more level districts between these various mountain ranges we meet with vast areas of fertile land, destined hereafter to become important agricultural and pastoral countries.

The whole of this part of British Columbia abounds in rivers and lakes. Among the latter the principal are, Lake Kamloops, Lake Shushwap, and Lake Okanagan. They are all situated in the midst of a country abounding in gold, and which may be termed the Lake District. These lakes, all of which receive a number of tributary streams, are fine sheets of water. Shushwap is about forty-five miles in length, and from five to ten in width. It is studded with islands, and situated in the midst of a rich pastoral country. Lake Okanagan, in an equally fine district, is a long, narrow sheet of water, running nearly due north and south; it is about eighty or ninety miles in length, by eight to ten in width. Its waters are deep, and well suited for navigation.

The greater number of the streams flowing through this part of British Columbia are tributaries of the Fraser. This celebrated river rises in the Rocky Mountains, and after flowing in a north-westerly direction for the first part of its course between two ranges of mountains, it gradually finds its way round to the south after passing Fort George in latitude 54° North. It now flows in a southerly direction for many hundred miles, the whole of which portion of its course is auriferous, until it reaches Fort Hope, when it makes a final bend to the westward, and falls into the Gulf of Georgia, close to the boundary line of the United States territory, to the north of the forty-ninth parallel of north latitude. A little below latitude 54° North it receives its northern branch, sometimes called Stuart's River, flowing into it from the north-east, after drawing its waters from a chain of lakes. The union of the two forms the Fraser River proper. Just below latitude 53° North it receives the Quesnelle River from the east.

This river consists of two branches, one of which drains the Quesnelle Lake, fifty miles in length, while the more northerly receives the surplus waters of the Upper and Lower Cariboo Lakes, one of which receives the Swamp River, and the other Keithley's Creek. The junction of the two branches of this river form the Quesnelle Forks, where a depôt for the supply of the Cariboo diggings has been established.

The Fraser River now flows past Fort Alexandria, to which I have already alluded; in that part of its course which lies between this point and its junction with the Thompson at Lytton, it receives a number of tributaries, none of which are of sufficient importance to merit a special notice, except the Chilcoteen and the Bridge River, both of which flow into it from the west. The latter river is rich in gold, and is therefore an exception to the rule that those rivers flowing into the Fraser from the east, are alone auriferous. Nodules of pure copper have also been found in the bed of this river.

The Thompson River is formed by the junction of two principal streams. The one flowing from the north rises in that chain of mountains whose opposite slopes form the water-shed of the Swamp River, and flowing in a southerly direction receives the waters of a variety of tributaries, some fed by chains of lakes, until it forms a junction at Fort Kamloops with the main branch of the Thompson, which flows out of Lake Shushwap, for whose surplus waters it forms an outlet. The river now flows through Lake Kamloops, which lake receives the Tranquille and Copper River, and finally falls into the Fraser at Lytton. Near the mouth the current is deep and rapid, and flowing between steep rocky banks. Before its junction with the River Fraser it receives the Nicaomen and the Nicola from the south, and the Bonaparte from the north, all of which drain the waters of a number of small lakes.

The Bonaparte is a stream rich in gold, and flowing through a fine arable country. The chief of the lakes whose waters flow into this river are Lakes Loon and Vert, both about twelve miles long. The Columbia River also rises in the British dominions, and, after flowing through a chain of lakes, crosses the southern boundary and enters the United States territory. It receives the united waters of the Okanagan and Similkameen, both flowing into it from British Columbia.

## CHAPTER XII.

Idea of an Inter-Oceanic Line of Railway—United States Line—Importance of such a Line of Railroad on British Territory—Circumstances favouring its Adoption—Great Advantages attending it—The Splendid Future it would open to British Columbia and Vancouver's Island—The Overland Route from St. Paul's, Minnesota, to British Columbia, by the Red River and Saskatchewan—Its Practicability discussed—The Country through which it passes—Probable Expense of the Journey—Routes followed by Mr. M'Laurin, in 1858 and 1860—Recent Accounts of Canadians about to undertake the Journey—Difficulties of crossing the Rocky Mountains—Letters in the "Times"—Company recently started for conveying Emigrants by this Route.

THE fratricidal war now raging in the United States, whatever be its issue, as regards the future political relations of the contending parties, cannot fail to exercise a most depressing influence on the commercial energy and enterprise of the country, and must, I fear, delay the completion of the inter-oceanic railway beyond the end of the present century. Such, at least, is my own opinion; at the same time we have seen that the House of Representatives has passed a bill, by a majority of thirty-two, to extend the railway and telegraph systems from the Atlantic to the Pacific.

"The bill incorporates a company, with seventy-five corporations, to construct a railroad from the one hundred and second degree of west longitude to the western boundary of Nevada; and grants to the company every alternate section of land on the line of the road, and also bonds of the United States to the amount of 16,000 dollars a mile. The Federal Government is to be represented in the company by five commissioners; public lands are granted, and the public credit loaned to the enterprise, the latter taking the shape of six per cent. bonds, of 1,000 dollars each, running thirty years. The route chosen is known as the "middle" route, namely, from Western Kansas to Western Nevada, and the Government engages to concede the railroads, now in course of construction through Kansas and California, such aid as may be necessary to their completion. And, as a return for such subsidies and grants, the usual preference is to be given to the Government in the transmission of troops and material, and in the use of the telegraph, which the company is also required to construct collateral with its road. Two years are given for the location of the track."

As I before remarked, however, I fear that the present moment is hardly likely to prove favourable to the execution of such a scheme; nay, I doubt much whether the present generation will witness its accomplishment; it is therefore natural that our thoughts should revert to the possibility of seeing this grand design carried to a successful issue on British territory.

The line of rail in the United States is at present open from New York, as far as St. Joseph's, Missouri. The remainder of the journey is performed in coaches, passing through the Mormon settlement of Utah, and so on to Sacramento and thence by water to San Francisco, on the Pacific. The pony express, whose arrival I witnessed at San Francisco, travels through the same tract of country. There is also a line of electric telegraph, extending the whole of the distance from one ocean to the other.

If the Americans were in a position to employ their resources in completing the inter-oceanic line of railway, the great stream of passengers and traffic would naturally flow in the channel that had been prepared for it, and it is doubtful whether any attempt to compete with it in Canada would be deemed likely to prove a remunerative speculation. As matters at present stand, however, I should like to see our own Government take the initiative in the matter, and, by completing this great work on British soil, confer an incalculable benefit on the whole of its colonies in North America.

The situation of British Columbia and Vancouver's Island, on the Pacific, is admirably adapted for carrying on a trade with China, Japan, India, and Australia, and it is not too much to suppose that these colonies must become the great highway for traffic between the above-mentioned countries and England, in the event of the completion of this line of railroad. The distance between London and Pekin would by this means be reduced some ten thousand miles, and the entire journey would probably not occupy more than a month or five weeks—while Vancouver itself would be brought some five or six thousand miles nearer to this country than even by the short overland route of Panama. Lastly, a considerable saving of time and distance would be effected, in the transmission of even the Australian mails, by this route over that of Panama. May we not therefore hope that the railway, now in progress between Halifax and Quebec, may be the first portion of a Canadian inter-oceanic railway, which shall, for ages to come, prove the great highway of communication between the east and the west.

I have more than once discussed the feasibility of this grand scheme with Colonel Moody, of the Royal Engineers—a question in which he felt great interest. His fixed idea always was that Burrard's Inlet, from its situation, depth of water, and other natural advantages, was destined to be the great emporium of commerce on the Pacific, at the western terminus of the railway. The natural harbour known as Burrard's Inlet is situated some few miles to the north of the mouth of Fraser River. Whether such a destiny be reserved for it or not, I think there can be little doubt that Esquimalt, with its noble and capacious harbour, will attract the attention it deserves, in the event of any such scheme being carried out.

What a grand future would the construction of such a line of railroad open for these remote dependencies of the British Crown on the Pacific! What a glorious day would that be for British Columbia when, vessels sailing from India, China, and Australia should meet at some point on her coasts, to land their passengers and discharge their cargoes, returning again laden with articles of our own manufacture! Numbers of those passengers to India, China, and Australia, who now go by way of the Cape of Good Hope, or by the present so-called overland route, *via* Marseilles and Suez, would in preference select the inter-oceanic railway of Canada, as both cheaper and more expeditious. The saving in the time of transit to China, especially to the more northern portions of that empire, and to Japan, would be very great, and the mercantile community, both in England and in the East, would be greatly benefited by the establishment of a constant, speedy, and safe means of communication passing through British territory. Of the advantages that must accrue to our own colony of British Columbia from the establishment of an emporium for the commerce of the West, which should not only vie with San Francisco, but eventually develop into the Liverpool of North America, it is unnecessary to insist on any farther.

Another great advantage to be derived from the establishment of a line of communication between the Atlantic and Pacific through British territory, would be the facilities it would afford for the transport of troops, stores, and artillery to any point along the frontier line, or on the coast of the Pacific, in the event of a war with the United States.

The great natural difficulty that would oppose itself to the execution of such a scheme would, no doubt, have to be overcome in the Rocky Mountains. At the same time I do not apprehend that this would prove an insuperable barrier to the engineering genius of our age. The results of the recent survey of Captain Palliser would seem to indicate that the difficulty is not so great as has been imagined, as a tunnel, at a certain spot, would reduce the extreme height to be crossed to 5,000 feet, which might be approached by gradients by no means unusual or excessive. This is no inconsiderable height to be traversed by a line of rail, it is true, but one which ought not, I think, to present an insuperable barrier to English skill and enterprise, after the example of the Sœmmering in Austria, and the Alleghanies in America, U.S.

An able correspondent of the *Times* comments in the following terms on the proposed line of interoceanic railway:—

"The advantages that would accrue to Great Britain from the entire service being performed through British territory are incalculable. The construction of the railway would not merely open to civilization a large territory in British North America, hitherto almost unexplored, but it would open up to the cultivators of the soil, in that territory and in Canada, a means of transit to all the markets of the Pacific, and an open passage to the China Seas, and to our possessions in the East Indies; in every aspect, whether viewed politically, socially, or commercially, the establishment of the proposed railway would give a progressive impulse to the affairs of the world, which, in its results, would eclipse anything that has been witnessed even amid the extraordinary achievements of the present century. That the railway will infallibly be made is as certain as that now is the time to undertake it; one does not require to be a prophet to predict that when the resources of British Columbia are fully opened up, and a communication established between the Atlantic and the Pacific, there will be enough traffic for a dozen steamers as large as the 'Great Eastern' on both oceans. The British Empire has now an opportunity of securing that position which it has hitherto occupied without dispute, as the greatest commercial nation in the world."

One other important fact must I point out in connection with this interesting subject ere we take leave of it. Assuming that Halifax is to be the Atlantic station of the line of railway, and some point on the coast of British Columbia the other terminus, on the Pacific, the neighbourhood of both these places abounds in coals—Nova Scotia on the one coast, and Nanaimo, Vancouver, on the other being the great coal-producing districts. This highly significant fact seems in itself to indicate the two points between which the inter-oceanic line of railway is destined to run.

Whatever be the case as regards the execution of this great scheme of an unbroken line of railroad from ocean to ocean, there can be no doubt that an attempt will be made to carry out the long-projected idea of an overland communication from Lake Superior by the Red River, Lake Winnipeg, and the Saskatchewan, to the foot of the Rocky Mountains, and finally, across them into British Columbia. The opening up of this route would not only confer an immense benefit on the last-mentioned place, but would tend greatly to develop the natural resources of the country through which it passes, which are evidently very great. The climate is by no means so severe as might be expected from the latitude, herds of buffalo being found as far north as parallel 60°. Indian corn ripens on the Saskatchewan. The rivers are free from ice in the beginning of May; wheat sown shortly after in the valley of the Red River may be gathered in the month of August. In addition to these natural advantages of soil and climate, gold is known to exist in the valley of the Saskatchewan, as well as in that of the Athabasca.

The overland route, *via* Canada and the Red River, can, according to the Toronto papers, be performed in about twenty days from that city, and at a cost of about 26*l*. All the necessary arrangements are now being perfected by a committee of gentlemen in Toronto, so that immigrants to the Fraser River and British Columbia may avoid the dangerous Panama route. From Toronto passengers will proceed to St. Paul and Minnesota by rail; thence to Red River by stage and steamboat. At that settlement they will be able to procure Indian guides and all other necessaries for making their way across the Rocky Mountains. This is no doubt the quickest and cheapest, and for those fond of adventure with a spice of danger, and who are not afraid to rough it, the pleasantest route to the diggings, if it be only practicable.

A correspondent writing to the *St. Paul's Press* in respect to the overland route, says that, with a propeller on Lake Winnipeg, and a river steam-boat on the Saskatchewan, the traveller could reach a point at the eastern base of the Rocky Mountains, not more than 100 miles distant from the eastern border of the Cariboo district, British Columbia, with every probability that the Saskatchewan gold-fields on the eastern slope of the Rocky Mountains will prove a counterpart to the diggings which have been opened on the other side. This would make the Fraser River diggings not more than five days' journey from the navigable waters of the Saskatchewan and Athabaska Rivers.

The *St. Paul's Pioneer*, of the 29th of April, announces the arrival there of a party of seventy Canadians, from Toronto and Hamilton, *en route* for British Columbia, by Fort Garry on the Red River and the Saskatchewan. It says: "We understand it is the intention of the party to go to George Town by Burbank's stages, then down the Red River on the steamer 'Fort Garry,' from thence to the Saskatchewan, and up that river to its head waters, whence they will continue their journey in ox-carts. If they find the diggings at the head of the Saskatchewan profitable, they will remain during the winter, otherwise they will push forward across the mountains to Cariboo mines, three hundred miles west of Fort Edmonton.

"These gold-hunters are a hardy and intelligent set of men, and go with a determination to succeed. They represent that other parties, to the number, probably of 150, will emigrate during the season to the Cariboo mines, taking the same route that they have mapped out.

"The emigrants now here had a meeting yesterday at the American House, and divided into parties of ten persons, the first detachment going off to-day, the others to follow daily by stage until they reach Red River."

A correspondent of the *Toronto Leader*, speaking of the overland route, and of the outfit and provisions necessary to be taken by travellers across the Rocky Mountains, writes:—

"The provisions should consist of flour, bacon, beans, tea, sugar, salt, pepper, soda, hard bread, and vinegar. As to the quantity of the above, each person may judge for himself. Cooking utensils may consist of camp-kettle made of sheet iron, straight up and down; the size will depend on the number of the party in one gang. Tea-pot, frying-pan, tin plates and knives, a tin dish to mix dough for baking, and tin cups. The diseases most prevalent are the scurvy and prairie itch. These may be prevented or cured by the frequent use of vinegar, and also black pepper. Many parties going are not aware of this, and in consequence suffer much from these maladies. The best kind of fire-arms are rifles; shot-guns are perfectly useless. Revolvers are also of little use, as you must not make too free in shooting an Indian by the way, even if you do get a chance; better bear with an insult than to stir up the ire of these savages. Also provide a tent, made of twilled cotton, and a strong shovel to dig a trench round the tent, to carry off the water in time of rain. Take one gold pan for prospecting, size twelve inches across the bottom, sixteen across the top, and five inches deep, made of sheet iron. Prairie matches, which can be always purchased in any store in Canada; they are much better than common matches. Mules are the best for packing, as they stand the heat much better and travel further than Indian ponies, and are not so apt to be stolen by the Indians, but are much more expensive on account of their having to be purchased from the whites. Oxen are the best for travelling with waggons. An ox-team can travel twenty-five miles per day, and are good to eat at the end of the journey. Whatever kind of beast you travel with should be shod before starting out, or else they will get foot-sore, which may cause a good deal of delay. You will require pack-saddles if you take mules; take lasso and pins to drive in the ground, to which the animals are to be tied at night. If you suspect Indians to be around your tent, you should keep sentry at night. to keep them from stealing your animals. If travelling with canoes, you should take oil-cloth to cover the provisions, to keep off water. As for clothing, common coarse clothes are most serviceable, strong boots, heavy-soled and well-nailed; light boots or mocassins are of no use. If you intend to buy ponies, buy from the Indians; you must take half-dollar pieces of silver as payment, as they use them for ornaments. Sugar is also much esteemed by the Indians; they will give a buffalo skin for a pint of sugar, which would be good for the boys to sleep on, as the nights are very cold on the mountains. High winds are very prevalent on the mountains, and if your tents are not properly secured, you may not think it strange to get it turned into an umbrella reversed, or balloon. The game are buffalo and antelope. Buffalo will be scarce in the spring, as it is far north, but should you shoot any, and wish to save the meat and make it light for carriage, you must jerk it over the coals, which is done in the following manner—drive four crotchet stakes in the ground, about eighteen inches high, put sticks across the crotches and cover over with green willows, then lay your meat on, and keep turning it over and over until it is pretty well cooked, and after being so treated it will keep any reasonable length of time. The antelope is a very shy animal, and hard to shoot; the only method is to tie a red handkerchief to the end of your ramrod and lie flat down in the grass yourself; holding up the handkerchief with the end of your ramrod, wave it slowly to and fro, at the same time not allowing your body to be seen above the grass. They seem to be attracted by the red handkerchief, and will come up within range, and by being expert you may chance to get a shot at them.

"The following seems to be a fair and liberal estimate of the expenses of the overland journey:—

|  | Dollars |
|---|---|
| From Toronto to St. Paul's (second class), with provisions, at least | 21 |
| St. Paul's to George Town, Burbank's stage | 25 |
| George Town to Fort Garry, steamer | 10 |
| Meals and lodgings, St. Paul's to George Town | 4 |
| Canoe, to hold eight persons, 32 dollars; for each | 4 |
| Horse, an inferior animal | 40 |
| Pack-saddle and bridle | 1 |
| Provisions, &c. | 20 |
| Incidental charges | 5 |
| Total | 130 |

"In the above I do not include expenses during detention at Fort Garry, nor payment for a guide, which would be requisite in ascending the Saskatchewan."

A Mr. M. Laurin, an old Californian miner, left St. Paul, Minnesota, for Fraser River, in July, 1858, and, after many adventures, reached his destination. Starting again thence from the Forks of Quesnelle, in the Cariboo country, on the 15th of August, 1860, he proposed to ascend the Fraser River to its source, and thence recross the mountains to the head waters of the Athabasca and Saskatchewan. His party consisted of four persons besides himself, their conveyance being a canoe. Reaching Fort George they ascended the semi-circular sweep of the Fraser River, which I have already described, when its course is deflected from the north-west to the southward, prospecting as they advanced. They were thus the pioneers in the discovery of the Cariboo country, bringing 1,600 dollars of its gold with them.

Leaving their canoe, where the river became unnavigable, they followed one of its branches, and passed through the "Leather Pass" in the Rocky Mountains, in lat. 53° N., reaching Jasper House, a Hudson's Bay fort, on the eastern side of the mountains, in a few days of easy travel on foot. From Jasper House to Fort Edmonton on the Saskatchewan, thence to Fort Garry, on the Red River of the North, and finally on to St. Paul on the Mississippi, was at that time a journey of 120 days in the French wooden carts, drawn by the oxen of the north-western plains.

We would advise no one to undertake the trip by this route to the diggings, unless he can reach his starting-point—St. Paul, Minnesota—with suitable clothing, and at least one hundred dollars in money. With rigid economy, and in organizations of four or five, or more, in a party, the overland journey to the Cariboo mines can be accomplished for that sum, according to received accounts.

Mr. M'Laurin—since deceased—was always accustomed to declare that a person landing at the mouth of the Fraser River would necessarily spend more money in reaching the gold mines of Cariboo than if St. Paul's on the Mississippi were his starting-point, and his route thence over the plains of the Saskatchewan and through the Leather Pass, in latitude 53°. However surprising this fact may appear I can credit it, knowing the high price of provisions and other necessaries of life in the gold countries. Assuming, therefore, that this is the case, we are forced to come to the conclusion that a great part of the expense of the voyage out to Victoria can be saved by any one who may possess sufficient energy and resolution to attempt the overland route to the gold mines of Cariboo, starting from St. Paul in the month of May, and following the familiar tracks of the Hudson's Bay traders.

From the foregoing accounts I think it may safely be concluded that no insuperable difficulties lie in

o

the way of the accomplishment of the overland route as far as the foot of the Rocky Mountains. It was at this point I always felt the real difficulties of the route would present themselves. In confirmation of the above opinion, I would beg to append a final extract from quite a recent number—April of this year—of the *Victoria British Colonist*. I hope my readers will not consider I have detained them too long in the discussion of the practicability of this route, but it is evidently a question in which very great interest is felt at the present moment, and the recent discussion in the *Times*, which arose out of the fact of the advertisement of a company having been formed for the conveyance of passengers to British Columbia by the overland route, shows the importance that is generally attached to this subject:—

"From Fort Garry to the Rocky Mountains we regard it only as a pleasure excursion for a company of young men with a good 'fit-out.' Where the difficulties will be encountered is in the Rocky Mountains, or from the passes through them till the settlements of British Columbia can be reached. If, for instance, a party of immigrants from Red River strike westwardly to Fort Carlton, then up to Fort Edmonton, from thence to Jasper House, then up the Athabasca to Miett's River, and up that to Tête Jaune, or Yellow Head Pass,* they could reach

* This is the pass traversed by M·Laurin, and called by him the "Leather Pass."

## DIFFICULTIES OF THE ROUTE.

the latter point, matters might go along first-rate. Even down as far as Tête Jaune Cache, at the head of canoe navigation on the east branch of the Fraser, a party could get along very well. But from the Cache, which is due east from the Cariboo mines, how are emigrants to proceed on to the settlements in the mines, or even to reach Fort George? We don't profess to be very well posted in the means of getting over that section of the route; yet we are persuaded that it is the most difficult to encounter by land of any part of the overland journey. We can very well understand that, if canoes could be had at Tête Jaune Cache, the journey down the Fraser to Fort George, to the mouth of Swift, or Quesnelle River, or Alexandria, might be made the easiest part of the whole route. But there is no guarantee whatever that canoes can be had there; if they can, whether enough can be had to transport any considerable number of immigrants down the river. If canoes cannot be had, as a matter of course a trail through a thickly-wooded country, along the banks of the river, would entail great hardships on the pioneers. If exhausted by the previous part of the journey, and withal short of provisions, some deplorable accident might occur.

"If immigrants, instead of taking the Yellow Head Pass, were to pass the mouth of Miett's River, continue up Athabasca River, and through the

Rocky Mountains, *via* the Committee's Punch-Bowl, and so on till they reached Canoe Encampment on Columbia River, how are they to reach the mines? If no canoes can be had, they will be forced either to follow down the banks of the Columbia to Fort Shepherd or Fort Colville—which will prove a very difficult journey—or cross from Canoe Encampment to North River or Lake Shushwap. The difficulties in reaching either of the latter places are doubtless very great, whilst that down the river by land would very probably be superior for immigrants, owing to the probability that many miners will find their way high up the Columbia from Colville this season. Yet the assistance they could afford would be very small. And if the immigrants did find canoes enough at Canoe Encampment—which we think improbable—they would have a long journey before them from Colville to Fort Kamloops on the Thompson, or Hope on the Fraser, both of which are a long way from the Cariboo mines. Both the entrances to British Columbia, whether by the Yellow Head Pass or the Committee's Punch Bowl, are beset with very serious difficulties in the way of the overland immigrant. As both those passes lead more immediately to the Cariboo mines than any of the southern routes, it is advisable that immediate steps be taken to render them passable, or at least in the intervening country between there and Cariboo a trail should be blazed * with directions that could not be mistaken. Indian guides might be had; yet even they could not render a land journey from either of those passes to Cariboo an easy matter, more particularly if exhausted and short of provisions. We have a positive interest in promoting overland travel; and as the primary destination of those who may come that way is in the mines, it would be very bad policy not to put ourselves to some trouble to render our part of the journey as easy and short as possible. For if an immigrant can reach Yellow Head Pass by the first of August, with an easy trail from there to Cariboo, he might spend six weeks or two months in the mines before being required to push his way south to winter quarters. Such an advantage would be a very great boon to the overland pioneer and the country generally.

" Except the Hudson Bay Company's people, no immigrant has yet entered British Columbia by the Yellow Head Pass or Committee's Punch Bowl. What immigrants have arrived, have struck south from the Saskatchewan to the boundary line, and have thence entered the colony either *via* Fort Colville and Portland, or *via* Fort Colville and Similkameen.

* This term signifies to open a new trail or path through a country. In its original acceptation it means indicating a path through a forest by cutting notches in trees.

"This southern route we believe to be the only safe one that can be recommended at present to the overland traveller. Yet it is bad enough, and brings the immigrant into the country so far from his destination—the that mines—it never can commend itself to any one, except as a choice between evils, the southern route being a lesser evil than the northern. Even Vermillion Pass, which is between the northern and southern passes, to which we have alluded, is beset, according to Palliser, with very great difficulties—too great, in fact, to be recommended—except it is improved by a trail connecting it with Shushwap Lake and Fort Kamloops.

"We have expressed some anxiety about the safe arrival of the overland pioneers this year. We feel that parties attracted to our mines, overland from Canada, moving for protection in large companies, and not inured to the trapper's life, or expert in his precarious mode of providing food, are very likely to run short of provisions, and may suffer severely in consequence. We have no doubt that the whole-hearted people of Cariboo would push forward supplies and assistance at any cost, should suffering immigrants require it; yet we think that something more is required. A catastrophe should be avoided, and consequently, if reliable guides can be sent out to intercept the immigrants, and conduct them by the shortest and safest way into the best portion of the country, it ought to be done. We feel persuaded that where we have now one person in the country who has crossed from Fort Garry to Fraser River, there will be tens of thousands within the next five years; and, as a matter of course, we cannot commence too early in opening the route or preventing accidents, and the Executive—who so well understands the merits of the subject—ought to commence forthwith."

I sincerely hope that the concluding hint with regard to sending out guides will receive the attention it deserves from the Colonial Government.

A correspondent of the *Montreal Gazette*, writing on the same subject, says:—

"To the strong and bold, and such as can paddle their own canoe, this route is perfectly practicable. Twice I have crossed the Rocky Mountains at the Old Columbia Pass, between Mounts Hooker and Brown Peaks, 16,000 feet in height— a majestic portal!"

This writer goes on to advocate a more northerly route to any to which I have yet drawn the reader's attention; as he says, the Rocky Mountains dip to where the Peace River gently winds its way across, along a break in the ridge, where few of the heights exceed 2,000 feet, and the country is comparatively smooth and only rolling.

"It was by this route that Sir Alexander M'Kenzie, in canoe from Montreal, struck the head waters of Fraser's River, and thence by water to the Pacific. What he, seventy years ago, did, may surely be done by others. However, great caution and thorough preparation would be necessary. Beyond a certain point, say Red River Settlement, or the mouth of the Saskatchewan, depôts of provisions—say pemican and flour, &c.—are out of the question—impossible. Of all routes, I would prefer that of Peace River, as overlapping from the *west* the broken base of the Rocky Mountains. It is, in fact, a canal to the Fraser—to the very head or heart, it may be, of the gold regions there. The route next south, crosses the mountains at a much higher elevation, and involves a heavy expenditure in horses—an article now of high price even there. This route is by a northern branch of the Saskatchewan, and strikes the celebrated 'Cariboo diggings.' Thompson's River—so called from our old townsman David Thompson—may also be thus reached. Many years ago I was there, but went by the Columbia—now, alas! no British stream! There was an empire thrown away! No party attempting any overland route should be of less than twelve nor more than eighteen, or at most twenty-four—divided into canoe crews of six to each, with one guide, an experienced *voyageur*, to each canoe, and at least one in the brigades should have some skill in surgery. No 'passengers' allowable, and every man to be equal to a three mile 'portage,' with a load of one piece—90 lbs.—regular *voyageurs* carry, yea, run with two such pieces, and in short portages even more. The route I would suggest is the north-west one, viz., by Pigeon River, Lake Superior. Say, steam to Pigeon River, thence by said route to the mouth of the Saskatchewan—there, and also *en passant* at the mouth of the Winnipeg, taking provisions— say pemican, flour, grease, &c.—to the utmost capacity of canoes—said provisions supplied in advance from Red River Settlement. From the mouth of Saskatchewan to Fort M'Leod, west of the Rocky Mountains, and on waters within '317 yards' of one of the head sources of the tree-like Fraser, there is continuous canoe navigation. Before me is Sir George Simpson's itinerary of the route in 1828. This part of the route took him—with his 'brigade' of two canoes, nine men to each—from 22nd July to 11th September, working, on an average, eighteen hours in the twenty-four; and that with picked men, not one of whom in the long, arduous, and at that time most perilous voyage from Hudson's Bay to the Pacific, including a blind, headlong dash, in small canoes and frailest craft, from the head to the mouth of the torrent Fraser—a three months' brush—gave up on the route, or, so far as appears from the very full journal of Chief Factor Archibald Macdonald, who accompanied the Governor, met with a single accident."

It will be seen from this extract that there are great and manifold advantages to be secured by the adoption of this northern route, as the mighty barrier presented by the Rocky Mountains ceases then to be formidable. The fact also of there being a continuous canoe navigation from the heart of the American continent to within 317 yards of one of the sources of the Fraser, is interesting and suggestive. Let us hope that fresh explorations may soon throw additional light on the advantages connected with the adoption of this route.*

The scheme of taking out a party from England to British Columbia by the great overland route is a bold one. In the present stage of its development, however, it must be regarded as beset with difficulties, but at the same time as deserving our best wishes for its ultimate success. The route selected by this company, as set forth in the advertisement, is by steam from England to Quebec, thence by the Grand Trunk Line of Canada and

* Those who may be interested in the question of the overland route generally, I would refer them to a small work on the subject, published by Professor Henry Youle Hind, of Trinity College, Toronto.

continuous lines of railway to Chicago and St. Paul's, and *via* the Red River Settlements, in covered waggons, to British Columbia. According to their programme one party at least must already have started, and are now following in the footsteps of those seventy Canadians to whom I have already referred, and whose arrival at St. Paul's, Minnesota, is chronicled in one of its papers. Any intelligence of their movements that may reach this country cannot fail to be interesting and important.* No doubt the passage across the Rocky Mountains will present the most serious difficulties they will have to contend with. At the same time, as a proof that I do not consider any obstacles they may present as insuperable, I can assure my readers that I had fully made up my mind to return to England by this route, and should have done so had not subsequent events compelled me to abandon my intention. In the case of my returning to these colonies, however, I shall hope to carry out

---

* An interesting account of the arrival of this party of immigrants in Canada appears in the *Times* of July 28. The Canadian papers express apprehension that due provision has not been made for so difficult a journey; they go on, however, to state that about 500 of the party have started on their distant and adventurous pilgrimage. Let us hope the Canadians will make it a point of honour, as it certainly is one of great interest and importance with them, to afford the travellers every assistance in their power, and do their utmost to ensure the successful issue of the enterprise.

my original intention, and I feel perfectly confident that but a very short time will elapse before this route is fairly opened for travelling. Whether our Government carry out the grand idea of an inter-oceanic railway on British soil or not, let us hope that they will lose no time in establishing a line of telegraph across this continent. As I entertain no doubt that the engineering talent of the present age will succeed in triumphing over the difficulties of the Atlantic Submarine Telegraph, this would establish an unbroken line of communication more than half round the globe, and a very few years would probably suffice to complete the circuit.

## CHAPTER XIII.

New Routes through the Interior of British Columbia—The Bentinck Arm Route—The Bute Inlet Route—Effect of opening up New Routes to Cariboo—Gold on the Stickeen River—Gold on the North and Tranquille Rivers—Gold on the Upper Columbia River—Importance of opening a Route through British Territory—Captain Venables on the Bill-Whoalla Route—Route through American Territory—Probable Rush to the Gold Fields of British Columbia from California—Diggings on the Salmon River—A Sketch of the Journey across North America, as formerly accomplished.

The question of opening up the interior of British Columbia is one of such paramount importance at the present moment, in consequence of the vast influx of immigrants which may be expected, not only this season, but for years to come, that I trust my readers will allow me once more to bring the subject under their notice. I have been at great pains to collect the latest information in connection with any new routes that may be projected, or are actually in the course of construction through British Columbia, being well aware that all such information cannot fail to be of the greatest value to the intending immigrant or gold-seeker. The result of my inquiries has convinced me that in no country on the Pacific coast is so great an amount of public enterprise shown at the present moment as in British Columbia. I have already described the two principal routes into the interior—the Harrison Lillooett route, through Douglas, and the route up the Fraser River, through Fort Hope, Yale, and Lytton, both leading to Fort Alexandria and the Cariboo country. I have also drawn attention to the line of road in the course of construction from Fort Hope into the Similkameen country. In addition to these, two fresh routes are about to be opened, the northernmost from the Bentinck Arm—an arm of the sea penetrating the coast from the Pacific, considerably to the north of Vancouver's Island— to some point on the Fraser, either at Alexandria or where the Quesnelle falls into it from the Cariboo country. The Bentinck Arm Company have obtained the right to construct a pack-trail and waggon-road between these points, with the privilege of collecting tolls for five years, at $1\frac{1}{2}$ cents per lb., and 50 cents per head for stock. The Company expects to push a trail through forthwith, and from the numerous parties that have crossed by the route, I believe it is entirely practicable, and will prove an able auxiliary in opening up to civilization the whole region west of Alexandria. It promises to become the means of reducing the price of goods in the northern mines, and I feel sure it will become an important route as soon as the interior fills with population. I shall not be surprised to find stages established winter and summer, with inns scattered along it at frequent intervals.

Another route has been projected, more to the southward, from Bute Inlet to Alexandria and Cariboo, by Mr. Waddington. It is said to be nearly twenty miles shorter than by the Bentinck route to Alexandria, and it is intended to strike the Fraser at a point where it is in contemplation to put on steamers to ply on the upper portion of its course.

A flat-bottomed, stern-wheel steam-boat is now being constructed at Fort Alexandria, for the Upper Fraser carrying trade. She will be 90 feet long, 17 feet beam, and $3\frac{1}{2}$ feet hold. The engines will have 12-inch cylinders and $3\frac{1}{2}$ feet stroke. It was expected she would be in running order in July this year. The name of the new boat will be the "Enterprise."

Mr. Waddington has obtained the exclusive right to collect tolls on the Bute Inlet pack-trail for five years, at $1\frac{1}{4}$ cents per lb., and 50 cents for animals; and if a waggon-road be constructed, the right to collect as high as five cents per lb. tolls.

The distance to be traversed on the Bute Inlet route is set down in the prospectuses of the Company at 241 miles, of which 83 are river and lake navigation, with only 158 miles of land-carriage, whilst the Bentinck Arm route is said to be 232 miles in length, of which 53 only are by river, with 178 miles of land travel. So far as reaching the Fraser from the coast is concerned, the Bute Inlet route has the advantage of being the shorter by twenty miles, while it is much more accessible from Victoria than Bentinck Arm. No doubt the practicability of both routes will be tested this season, and the competition between them will facilitate the cheap transmission of goods to the northern mines, for as soon as both routes are in full operation, no doubt the rate of tolls will be diminished.

It is intended to open another route *via* Yale Lytton, and Bonaparte, to a point where it is intended to intersect the waggon-road from Lillooett to Alexandria. This route will connect the Cariboo country with the vast area watered by the Thompson and its tributaries, one of the richest agricultural and pastoral districts in British Columbia.

The moment that the interior and coast lines of

road are fully opened to stages and waggons an entire revolution will be wrought in British Columbia. The long distance to Cariboo, short supplies and high prices, will no more be heard of, and an era of prosperity and wealth will dawn on British Columbia such as the original trappers of the Hudson's Bay Company when they first followed an Indian trail through the dense forests of this unexplored region would have looked upon as a wild dream, whose realization could never be hoped for.

It will be seen that all these different lines of road tend to the great centre of attraction, the "El Dorado" of Cariboo; at the same time I entertain no doubt but that sooner or later, other districts will be discovered as rich or richer in their yield of the precious metal. Bands of prospectors have this spring started for the north with the view of exploring the Stickeen River, and from former accounts we have received, I anticipate rich discoveries in that region. I am persuaded, moreover, that there are other portions of British Columbia, not so distant as Stickeen, or even Cariboo, that are worthy the attention of the hardy and adventurous miner. There is a vast district drained by the North River and its tributaries, falling into the Thompson, a district, from all we can learn, that promises to be another Cariboo. This important stream to which I have already alluded, is the principal tributary of the Thompson, uniting

P

with that river in its course between Lake Shushwap and Lake Kamloops at the Hudson's Bay Fort of Kamloops. There can be no doubt that this river and all its tributaries are more or less auriferous, especially those flowing from the east, rising in the same range of mountains as the Cariboo streams; gold having already been found on various portions of the North River.

On Tranquille River, which falls into Lake Kamloops near North River, gold in considerable quantities has been found; consequently, it is quite natural to infer that the whole country is auriferous. The accessibility of this section of country at any season of the year, and the advantage of working claims at the diggings longer than at the northern mines, renders the whole of this country one of the most promising in British Columbia. Supplies can be sent by boat from Lake Kamloops up the river for one hundred miles, as far as the district in which a very fine specimen of coarse gold was found last summer in the bed of the river. The country in the immediate neighbourhood, moreover, contains some of the finest grazing and agricultural land in British Columbia, which I have already pointed out as lying in the immediate neighbourhood of the Lake district, as I termed it. The cost of living would not, in consequence, be anything like so high as it is in Cariboo.

From the northern tributaries of the North

River it is but a short distance to the Columbia River and Canoe Creek, which falls into the Columbia at the head of boat navigation. I have already in the preceding chapter alluded to the auriferous wealth of that portion of the Columbia River which flows through British territory. There can be no doubt it flows through a district rich in mineral deposits, and, if my information be correct, companies of prospectors will leave Colville and ascend the Columbia in boats, as the Hudson's Bay Company's *voyageurs* have been in the habit of doing. They will, in all probability, be the pioneers in the discovery of the rich and extensive gold fields drained by the north branch of the Columbia. It is desirable, for every reason, that the route to this country should lie through British Columbia, and not *via* Colville, or *via* the Dalles and Walla-Walla in American territory. From the best sources of information at our command, we learn that there is a practicable trail to the gold regions of Columbia *via* Thompson's River. Parties going there may either ascend North River and strike up one of its tributaries to cross the range dividing it from the Columbia, or may ascend the Thompson at the east end of Shushwap Lake and cross over from one of the streams that debouch into the lake.

It is a matter of considerable importance not only to Victoria and the towns on the Fraser as far as Lytton, that the country should be explored for a good practicable trail from the Thompson to the Columbia, as the travel and traffic would be kept in our colony instead of falling into the hands of our territorial neighbours.

I understand that Mr. Cox, Gold Commissioner at Rock Creek, has been instructed to supply the prospectors with provisions at Government expense for exploring the Okanagan country as far as Shushwap Lake, as well as the country west of Rock Creek. If the Government will not offer large rewards for the discovery of gold on the North River, or on the Columbia, the course taken by Mr. Cox will no doubt have a good effect. Every inducement ought to be held out to prospectors to open up the regions referred to, as the discovery that they were rich in precious metals, would tend greatly to advance the material prosperity of the colony, and I think there can be no doubt, from all the information we have received respecting them, that these regions will be found to possess auriferous deposits as rich or richer than any other, even in the land of gold—British Columbia.

The following communication from a friend of mine, Captain Venables, with whom I have often discussed the future prospects of British Columbia, and addressed by him to the *Victoria British Colonist*, I have taken the liberty of quoting, as it throws additional light on the project, already adverted to, of opening a route through the colony from Bentinck Arm:—

"As the time approaches when miners will be thinking of starting again for Cariboo and the Upper Fraser, a few remarks and suggestions on a route to those places which must eventually, when known, become one of great importance, may not be considered out of place. Should any at this time meditate trying the Bill-Whoalla trail by way of experiment, the little information I have been able to pick up during four months' residence there may be of use to them; and if others should be induced, from motives of economy in either time or money, to make a similar attempt, a little information would be to them perhaps equally acceptable.

"The road becomes open and practicable for animals in the beginning of April; in fact, some who propose to reach the Fraser by that route intend to start in March. The snow, at Bill-Whoalla itself, fell on the 28th of November, and has since averaged sixteen inches. The snow on the main plateau, fifty miles above Bill-Whoalla (by Narcoontloon and Chilcoten), is from six inches to a foot in depth, and disappears early. This I learn from Indians, who are constantly coming down and returning without snow-shoes. A large party of the Aunghim Indians, one of whom acted as my guide on every expedition, came down a week before Christmas, and returned on the 2nd or 3rd of January. The only place where snow may be expected will be near the banks of the Fraser.

"The absence of any houses of entertainment on the road will at first necessarily be considered a great drawback; but considering the short time, comparatively speaking, the journey takes, together with what might be done to mitigate this evil at the outstart, I think the advantages would outweigh the inconvenience. The Bill-Whoalla Indians are very friendly, and so are the other tribes round about. They are only too anxious for white men to come amongst them. They are mostly fine strong men, and are ready and eager to be employed in packing to the mines. I have been constantly among the Indians of the different tribes, and they are continually asking if the Boston and King George men are coming. They would gladly pack, I imagine, to the mouth of Quesnelle River or Alexandria for ten or twelve cents, and be then well paid. At the outside the journey would be ten days; a man could easily walk it without a pack in seven days.

"My suggestion would be—let a man take up sufficient provisions for the road, or if he wishes to avoid the heavy outlay which a poor miner must experience before he has struck a claim, let him take sufficient to last him three or four weeks, and pack one, two, or three Indians as the case may be. I assure him he will find no difficulty in procuring Indians. Nootlioch (Indian ranch) is thirty miles up the river; for fifteen miles above this goods can be taken in small canoes. Narcoontloon is thirty miles—a good road, with the exception of one bad hill (the slide). Here there is another Indian ranch, from which it is fifty miles to Chilcoten (Indian rancherie), good trail, perfectly level. From there it is sixty miles to Alexandria, or about seventy miles to the mouth of Quesnelle River. The trail from the top of the Nootlioch hill is, for foot passengers, as good the whole way as any part of the Brigade trail, with the exception of one or two places where there is a little fallen timber. The trail follows a chain of lakes, and could, consequently, if taken straight, be made much shorter, and also avoid much soft ground. Game and fish are abundant on the road. I caught several trout with a string, a small hook, and a grasshopper on my way down. The Aunghim and Chilcoten Indians have a good many horses, which might be turned to use for packing.

"My remarks only refer to this road as it is; and as I think it may be made useful this year, I wish to say nothing as to what might be made of it. If it is of any value, the miners will themselves discover it to be so, and in that case it *must* eventually become of importance. I can only say that we brought our horses down packed, and that there are now four horses at Bill-Whoalla. At the same time numerous animals travelling on the trail in its present state would soon render it impassable in some places.

"I must say a few words of the Bill-Whoalla Indians. Since I have been there, they have in every way been kind and friendly. Although we often have nothing to give in exchange, they always supplied us with fish and game when they found we were really pressed for provisions. The old chief Pocklass went out purposely to shoot for us, and brought back twenty deer. When we left to get provisions he made us promise to return, and so to the last they were ready in every way to oblige us. They have seen less of white men than the other tribes, and it is a great pity that they should, like the others, be spoiled by the poison which is continually sold on that coast. About every fortnight small schooners pass up that way, calling at most of the Indian villages, and leave their mark behind. In almost every instance from 300 to 400 gallons of liquor is part of the cargo; not even wholesome liquors, but large five-gallon tins of alcohol—sometimes even mixed with camphine. In one instance the master of the craft was going to trade the pure liquor in the unbroken tin to the Bill-Whoalla Indians, but was prevented. They have very little liquor, and would have drunk it off pure as it was. I have been informed at Fort Rupert that the sale of alcohol is this year carried on to a greater extent than ever before, and it certainly is ruining any good qualities the Indians may possess. You generally find them at the ranches half-drunk. When I arrived at Fort Rupert some three weeks ago, I do not believe there were twenty sober men in the whole camp. This is an evil that might, I should think, be easily put a stop to."

It will be seen from the tenor of my preceding remarks on the gold-fields of the North River, the Lake District, Rock Creek, and the Upper Columbia, that I regard it as more than probable that new gold-mining districts are likely to be discovered in these parts of British Columbia, that may very probably prove a formidable rival to the celebrated diggings of Cariboo. All the accounts we have received from these regions seem to warrant that conclusion. As I before mentioned, the upper part of the course of the Columbia River may be reached through American territory, *via* Portland, the Dalles, Fort Vancouver, and Fort Colville, partly by water and partly by land; at the same time I hope our own Government will see the necessity of opening a route to this fine country through British territory.

While on the subject of routes, British and

American, I must not omit to mention that the *Puget Sound Herald* has an article in favour of the Puget Sound and Columbia River Railroad. The cost of constructing the road is estimated at 30,000 dollars a mile, making a capital of 2,400,000 dollars for the estimated distance of eighty miles. The *Vancouver Island Colonist*, in remarking upon this article, says:—

"The *Herald* favours Fort Vancouver just above the mouth of the Willamette as the best terminus on Columbia River, although Monticello, some distance below, is nearer to Olympia. Whatever may be the primary object of the projectors of this line of road, whether to secure a right in advance of the times on which to realise—whether to help the town of Vancouver, the ambitious rival of Portland, or whether to make Olympia the *entrepôt* for Washington and Oregon—whatever may be the object of the projectors, there can be no doubt that a railroad will ultimately be constructed connecting Puget Sound with Columbia River. We have long regarded its construction as a mere matter of time. The difficulties in crossing Columbia River Bar are such as can never be removed in the present state of engineering science. The freezing up of the river in winter is another very serious objection to its being the sole entrance to the great country drained by the Columbia. The Straits of Fuca and Puget Sound, with a railroad to the

Columbia, offer the safest and most certain means of entering the heart of what must ere long become a very populous country."

A letter from Victoria, Vancouver, in the *Toronto Leader*, after commenting on the severity of the past winter, and describing the damage done by the floods in Oregon and California, goes on to speak in the following terms of the probable rush to the diggings of British Columbia from the United States territory:—

"All this is not without its effect on us here, for last summer it was almost fabulous to see the amount of gold taken out of the mines by some men in the space of a few weeks. These men have been in California this winter, spending their money, and have created such an excitement among those injured by the floods, that an emigration of forty thousand to our mines is already commencing, and, if the excitement should continue, a much larger number than I have mentioned will come. Every individual arriving on these shores assists in developing the resources of the country, and to facilitate immigration, our Legislature have this year subsidized a steam-boat company to make one trip a week from San Francisco to this port. The last three boats have each brought up about 500 men.

"Now that we have opened mines of copper, coal, and silver, these men need no longer leave the country immediately on the termination of the gold-washing season, but can find profitable employment in the mines of the baser metals.

"This dreadful American war is not without its effects on this coast, for many wealthy Americans are quietly retiring their means from California and Oregon, and investing in these colonies. Our trade with China is also becoming daily more developed, as well as general business, in consequence of the operations of the Morrill tariff, and the three months' bonded system of the United States. The recent developments on the Amoor and Japan are also commencing to show the importance of this point to Great Britain, as an emporium for her manufactures to supply this coast and the North Pacific countries generally."

At the same time, I think it right to inform my readers that the Americans say they have found a rival for Cariboo in the Salmon River, on their own side the boundary line, in Washington territory, where, according to the accounts they give, immense gains have been realized. If this really be the case, as these mines open up earlier in the season, it is probable that most of the Californians may be induced to tarry here while they try their luck. This will, perhaps, be rather beneficial than not, as, if they crowd up *en masse* to Cariboo, it is doubtful whether there will be pack-animals sufficient to supply them with provisions.

I fear those of my readers who may not be specially interested in the question will be somewhat wearied of my description of routes, possible and impossible, across British Columbia and the American continent. Before taking leave of the subject, however, for good, I will give a brief sketch of the manner in which this journey was performed—in days which may now almost be regarded as gone by—by the Hudson's Bay traders, or any occasional traveller whom a love of sport or adventure may have induced to brave the dangers of this then almost unknown and unexplored route. Having, in the first instance, procured a letter of recommendation to the different factors commanding the forts, on the line of country he is to traverse, from Sir George Simpson, the late respected Governor-General of the Company, who was accustomed himself to travel from the eastern to the western settlements of the Hudson's Bay traders on his tours of inspection, we will suppose our party have reached their starting-point of Fort Garry on the Red River. The first step to be taken would be to procure a sufficient number of horses to convey themselves and their baggage across the wide plains of the west. Their horses are purchased of Indians, in good condition, and are laden with the necessary stores, such as food, spirits, and ammunition, either brought with our *voyageurs* from Halifax, or supplied from the forts. Guides, generally French-Canadians, having been engaged, the party set out on their three months' trip. At the end of a week or so they would probably reach one of the many stations of the Company, where they would remain to refresh themselves and their cattle before again setting out. At the termination of another similar period, after having crossed several streams, been exposed to storm and sunshine, and encountered many of the other vicissitudes of travel in these regions, they would once more come upon one of the isolated Hudson's Bay Forts, weary and travel-worn, and right glad to avail themselves of the generous hospitality always proffered by the hardy tenants of these "oases" of the wilderness. After another halt, and after having exchanged their now somewhat worn and foot-sore horses for others in better condition and more fit for service— an exchange which is however always one of mutual advantage, as, while it on the one hand provides the travellers with fresh horses, it serves on the other to introduce new blood among the stock of the Hudson's Bay traders, a matter of absolute necessity in these prairies,—they would once more pursue their journey. This, with occasional *rencontres* with Indians, of whom, if proper discretion, judgment and forbearance be displayed in our dealings with them, very little danger is, in most cases, to be apprehended, would constitute the leading features of such a journey. When our travellers had reached some point where they could transfer themselves and their effects in canoes, or any other conveyance by water to the coast, they were accustomed to dispose of their horses, and the real difficulties and hardships of the journey were virtually over. In the event of my returning to British Columbia, I shall endeavour to carry out a long-cherished project of crossing the American continent in this fashion. I should probably make for Fort Vancouver, on the Columbia River, and on reaching Portland, either take the first steamer to Victoria, or make my way across to Puget Sound, whence there is seldom much difficulty in getting conveyed by water to Vancouver.

# CHAPTER XIV.

We leave Victoria for San Francisco—Wells Fargo's Agency—The Mirage—A Modern "Robinson Crusoe"—Yankee Habits—Columbia River — Portland — We strike on a Rock—The Water gains on us in spite of all our Efforts—Critical Situation of the Steamer "Pacific"—We run her ashore—Portland—Picturesque Scenery on the Columbia River—San Francisco—Its Harbour—Description of the Town—Mexican Drovers—The Firemen of San Francisco—Effect of the Gold-Fever—Japanese Embassy—American Driving — Race-course—American Opinion of a Fox-Hunt—The "General" Drinking Bars—Theatres—Union Club—The "Pony Express"—The Chinese in San Francisco—The Vigilance Committee.

On the occasion of my final departure from the colony of Vancouver's Island, I took passage on board the mail-steamer that calls twice a month at Esquimalt for San Francisco. Wells Fargo's agent, as usual, formed one of the number of passengers, and he might be seen sorting his pile of letters and parcels, preparatory to his arrival at

San Francisco. The object of Wells Fargo's Agency is the safe and speedy transmission of letters and small packages throughout all the countries lying on the Pacific seaboard of the North American continent, consequently, they have their agents travelling along all the principal routes into the interior, and they have also established depôts or post-offices, as well as banking offices in all the principal towns. The travelling agent for British Columbia, Mr. Bellew, is a man of great courage and resolution. It is his habit, at intervals, so completely to disguise his personal appearance as almost to defy recognition. I have seen him at one time bearded like a Turk, at another close-shaven as a Puritan divine, now adorned with long flowing locks, now close cropped as a roundhead. His object in so doing is to render his identification as difficult as possible, as, being frequently entrusted with large quantities of gold, he thinks it desirable that his person should not be too well or too generally known.

I remember on the present occasion, in running through the Straits of Fuca, being struck with the singular effects produced by a natural phenomenon we had often observed previously. I mean the mirage. I have seen perfect and unbroken reflections, in the atmosphere, of such objects as churches, houses, ships, and trees, which were themselves distinctly visible as well as their reflected images.

Q

The effect of the double picture—the reality and its simulacrum—the upper one being, of course, inverted—was exceedingly singular and striking. We saw the Race rocks and their lighthouse under this aspect. The image of the reflected lighthouse seeming to point downwards, and to rest on the summit or apex of the real one. To one other atmospheric phenomenon of very frequent occurrence in these regions I will allude before taking leave of them. I refer to the brilliant meteors so commonly observed on fine nights, especially during the summer months.

An old friend of mine in the colony happened to be a fellow-traveller with us on the present trip, and we contrived to while away a considerable portion of time in discussing the details of an adventure that befell him, on the occasion of a former voyage in the year 1857, when on his passage from San Francisco to Australia. The vessel in which he sailed happened to put into one of the Navigator Islands, for yams, fresh vegetables, and fruits; the crew of one of the native canoes engaged in supplying them offered to take any of the passengers on shore who might like to see something of the island, while the ship lay off. My friend was the only person on board who availed himself of the offer; he, however, at once leaped into the canoe and was paddled ashore— having, at the same time, nothing on but a shirt and a pair of cotton trousers. Soon after he landed, a tropical squall happening to spring up, he was not surprised to see the ship put about and stand out to sea. This did not cause him any surprise or uneasiness, as he felt sure that, as soon as the squall had subsided, she would return and fetch him.

In this expectation he was however doomed to be disappointed, as the wind carried the vessel so far out to sea that she was wholly unable to make the island again, at least he concludes this must have been the case, as he certainly never set eyes on her again. He was thus left like a second Robinson Crusoe, a solitary man on the island of Toutouila, one of the Navigator group, in the midst of the Pacific. Assuming the practical wisdom of the maxim which sets forth the expediency of doing at Rome as the Romans do, he proceeded to act upon it by making himself as much at home and as comfortable as circumstances would permit, among the fortunately friendly savages with whom his lot had been so strangely cast, endeavouring, as far as possible, to conform to their habits and mode of life.

He had no reason to complain, from the very first, of the treatment he experienced at their hands, and the very high esteem in which he soon came to be held, was shown by his being elected a chief. Fortunately one of the natives had served for some time on board a whaler, and had managed to pick up a few words of English; he was therefore enabled to use him as an interpreter.

He spoke of the climate as being delightful, while delicious tropical fruits were produced in abundance. His health, he declared, was never better than during this compulsory sojourn on the island of Toutouila, a circumstance he ascribed in great measure to the regular life he led, and the simple wholesome food that formed his daily sustenance; not that this consisted solely of a vegetable diet however, the bill of fare was agreeably diversified by chicken and pork, both fowls and pigs—the progeny of a stock left here by Captain Cook—being found in abundance on the island.

After a sojourn of fully nine months another vessel, also bound for Australia, happened to put in, and, as may be supposed, he lost no time in claiming acquaintance with his kindred; the thoroughly savage guise, however, in which he went on board would almost seem to render any attempt at so doing an unwarrantable act of presumption on his part. Unkempt, unshaven, and clad in garments of primeval simplicity—his original clothes having long since fallen off in rags—he was, nevertheless, not aware that there was anything at all unusual in his appearance, so entirely had his present mode of life become a second nature. Nor was he impressed with this fact until the precipitate retreat of the ladies forced upon him the recollection that it is unusual for a gentleman to make his appearance on the quarter-deck in a condition so nearly approaching what the Latin poet would have described as "simplex munditiis." In spite of his savage appearance and ways, he nevertheless ultimately succeeded in making good his claim to brotherhood with the white men, and was taken with them to his original destination—Australia.

On the occasion of both my visits to San Francisco, we had a good many Yankee fellow-passengers on board our steamer. The greater part of their time was spent in playing the games known as Poker and Euker, accompanied by drinking, smoking, and chewing. Of all the methods of consuming tobacco the latter is surely the most objectionable, on account of the amount of spitting it necessitates. On more than one occasion they succeeded in fairly spitting me out of the cabin.

Our second trip, the one I am now describing, on board the mail-steamer "Pacific," was diversified by a visit to Portland, when we unfortunately came to grief in the Columbia River, in the manner I shall hereafter relate. There is always a very heavy, nasty sea on the bar of the river, the passage over which is, in every case, more or less difficult and dangerous. Steamers intending to go up this river always carry a pilot for that especial purpose. There is a light at the entrance to the Columbia River. Its current, especially during the spring and summer months, is very rapid, as its waters are then swollen by the melting of the snows in the Alpine regions where it takes its rise. After passing Astoria, the port of entry, about ten miles from the mouth, we at length reached Portland, 110 miles further, and situated on a bend in the river, very nearly at the limit of steam navigation for sea-going vessels. Portland is the great emporium of the inland trade of Oregon, Washington territory, and to a great extent British Columbia.

We left Portland on a beautiful starlight night, perfectly calm, but the current running strong, and we steaming at a considerable pace through the water. Nearly all the passengers had turned in, myself among the number, when I was suddenly aroused by being precipitated against the lower bunk board of my bed, everything in the cabin being at the same time shaken out of its place by the concussion.

Hastening on deck, I found we had struck on a rock well known in the Columbia River, and called the "Coffin Rock." Fortunately we had a very small freight on board, not having shipped more than fifty tons at Portland. Had we been heavily laden, and consequently deeper in the water, we must inevitably have sunk at once. As it was, the water gained on us with sufficiently alarming rapidity, pouring through the bows of the vessel in a stream as thick as a man's arm. After great difficulty, we got a sail over her bows, which stopped the leak to some extent, but very slightly. The pumps, being in excellent condition, did their work well, with the assistance of the donkey engines, and several extempore pumps rigged for the occasion. In spite of all our efforts, however, we had the mortification of finding the water continue to gain upon us, and our position, in fact, began to assume a most critical aspect, water-logged as we were on this tremendous current, in the middle of the night. The steamer soon commenced to lurch and roll in a frightful manner, and as we had a number of Chinamen on board, I made it my duty to set them to run *en masse* across the deck, from side to side, to bring her to after each roll; using them, in fact, as so much shifting ballast.

Soon after came a report that the water had gained the " engine room;" now it reached the men's ankles, now their knees, now their waists. Captain Staples, whose idea it had been at first to make for some spot where she would be pretty comfortably berthed, felt at this juncture that matters had become sufficiently serious for him to put her head straight for the bank, as we must inevitably have sunk like a piece of lead as soon as our fires were extinguished. This actually occurred just as we touched the bank, by which time the men in the engine-room were working up to their arm-pits in water. Our vessel keeled over on the bank, until it was impossible to keep one's footing on deck; meanwhile, Wells Fargo's agent lost no time in landing the letter-bags and other property in his charge. His example was soon followed, the boats were got out, and we sent the women and children on shore, a step which, in my humble opinion, ought to have been taken before.

Early in the morning we sent a boat up to Portland, informing them of our position; meanwhile, we had encamped, after a fashion, on shore, and tried to make ourselves as comfortable as we could, under the circumstances, until the arrival of the steamer from Portland. I forgot to mention that we lost a number of horses, as we had to throw them all overboard, and those that did not succeed in swimming on shore were drowned. On arriving at Portland, we spent our time, notwithstanding the great heat, chiefly in shooting and fishing. We contrived to find some very fair grouse-shooting at some distance from the place, and this, with some nice trout, provided us with a capital addition to our hotel fare. Portland can boast of possessing a very good race-course.

The scenery on the Columbia River, above Fort Vancouver, is of the most picturesque character. The celebrated Dalles is a mountain district through which the river winds its way in many a graceful bend, while Mount Hood, towering above all, may be distinguished, from various points of its course, between Astoria, Portland, and Fort Vancouver. I have beheld its snow-clad summit floating like a cloud above the distant horizon, while all below was hidden in a shroud of purple vapour; again have I seen it stand forth, in all its naked majesty, a gigantic pyramid of dazzling white, relieved against the deep blue sky.

The next mail-steamer calling at Portland proved to be the "Cortes," on which vessel we took our passage to San Francisco. This place, the chief city and port of California, we reached, after three days' passage from Portland.

San Francisco stretches along the shores of a bay of great size; so large indeed is it that it scarcely offers a safe anchorage for vessels in a high gale of wind. It always gave me the idea of a place trying to force its way into the sea, elbowing the waves, in fact, out of their lawful domain, and disputing for his realms with old Neptune. For years past San Francisco has been steadily encroaching on the water. The sea once came up to what is now the centre of the town, and ships used to discharge their cargoes in the midst of what is at present a closely built, densely populated neighbourhood. A great portion of what formerly constituted the harbour has been filled up and built upon; while in other places, edifices of every description are pushed out on piles. In fact, a great part of San Francisco is built in this manner, many of its principal wharves and warehouses resting on piles, the thoroughfares among which are often very dangerous, on account of the wooden pavement having rotted into holes. As San Francisco carries on a trade with almost all parts of the globe, vessels sailing under every flag are always to be seen in numbers on the bay, which presents in fine weather a very cheerful and enlivening *coup d'œil*. The town is of considerable extent, being by far the most important and populous American city on the Pacific.

The streets are all built at right angles to each other, as is generally the case in America. A great part of the town is built of wood, and we observed in some of the parts first built, as, for instance, in Battery-street, several of the old iron houses still standing, erected by the first settlers, who were attracted hither by the discovery of gold in 1848-9, long before the present town had sprung into existence.

Herds of cattle are frequently driven through the streets of San Francisco, as, in addition to what is consumed in the city itself, great quantities are exported. The animals are generally of the somewhat small Spanish breed I have already spoken of, and are more than half wild. The Mexican drovers in charge of them are all mounted, as they often come from great distances, and the cattle are generally too tired to be troublesome, by the time they reach San Francisco. Should any of them, however, prove restive, it is very curious to witness the dexterous manner in which these wild-looking, picturesque drovers, with their large embossed Mexican saddles and heavy stirrup-irons, will throw the lasso, and sometimes catching them by the horns, sometimes by the leg, will suddenly bring them to the ground with the most perfect ease and grace, and soon reduce the most wild and obstinate beast to a state of passive obedience.

Fires are of very frequent occurrence in San Francisco. During the brief period of our stay, at least two fires of considerable magnitude, and involving great loss of property, took place. The organization of the different corps of firemen in San Francisco is deserving of a few words of special notice. They constitute a really well-trained, able, and efficient body of men, and are all volunteers. There is another class whose office it is to attend on the fire brigade, following them wherever they go. These are called Hook and Ladder-men, and are very useful in protecting life and property. The city is divided into a number of wards, each of which contains certainly one if not two engine-houses; these are provided with a bell sufficiently loud-toned to make itself heard over the two or three surrounding wards; each one takes up the tocsin, and thus the first alarm of fire is conveyed almost instantaneously throughout the entire city.

In the event of a large fire, the great alarm-bell of San Francisco will strike a certain number of times, indicative of the number of the district in which the fire is to be sought. The firemen are, generally speaking, a fine body of young men, and their working dress is both appropriate and becoming. It consists of a red shirt and trousers, a belt, and a helmet—the latter indicating which corps the men belong to, such as "First or Second Tigers," and other fanciful names.

The fire-engines are generally perfect models of their kind, being beautifully light, and in many cases handsomely fitted in silver, and the firemen appear to take no small pride in them. The larger fire-engines, worked by steam, are capable of hurling an immense body of water against a conflagration, sending forth a stream like a column. A San Franciscan fireman, however engaged, or in whatever place he may be, is bound the moment he hears the fire-bell to don his red shirt and helmet and be off to the scene of action, the object of the organization being the mutual protection of property.

During the height of the British Columbia gold fever in 1858, people rushed in such masses from San Francisco to the diggings, that the town appeared as if it must be deserted, and land was sold for almost anything it would fetch. After the first excitement had passed away, however, things soon found their old level, and land that at that time was parted with for 1,000, is now worth 10,000 dollars.

During the period of my first sojourn at San Francisco, the different members of the same Japanese Embassy who have since attracted so much interest and attention in Europe, were stay- at the same hotel with me, the "International." They had recently arrived from Hakadadi, on their way to Europe *via* Panama and New York. I have frequently dined at the same table with them, and recently recognized the features of more than one of their number in the streets of London.

A bazaar containing a variety of curious and often really tasteful specimens of Japanese art and manufacture was open during my stay here. Some of the embroidered work was very elaborate and beautiful. I purchased several of the productions of this singular country, the fact of whose quaint yet genuine civilization was unmistakably impressed on many of the articles here exposed for sale.

I have already alluded to the wooden pavement of San Francisco. This applies not only to the foot- path, or side-walk as the Americans term it, but to the carriage road, which consists of planks, often rotten and loose, and giving a stranger the impres- sion of being highly dangerous.

In spite, however, of the defective state of the

roads, the Americans manage, in their one or two-horse buggies, to get over the ground with considerable rapidity; the pace being, indeed, somewhat startling to a novice, who is almost shaken to pieces by the continual jerking and bumping to which he is subjected in driving over the uneven and treacherous plank pavement of an American town.

The rules of driving, as regards the side of the road to be kept, are just the reverse of our own, being the same as those which hold good in Germany. The system of driving also, one would imagine, is calculated to destroy the mouth of any horse in the world. An American Jehu, before the ostler has let go the horse's head, will prepare for the coming struggle by twisting each rein three or four times round his wrist. When once off it seems to be a regular tussle between man and horse which shall pull hardest, whether the latter shall be hauled bodily backwards into the buggy, or whether the driver shall be pulled off his seat on to the neck of the quadruped.

Before quitting the subject of driving in America, I will ask my readers to accompany myself and some friends while we pay a brief visit to the San Franciscan race-course, a very respectable specimen of its kind, being a circular course exactly one mile round. We went to see a trotting match, what we should term a race being known as a running match. One of the chief difficulties in a race of this description, is to prevent the horse from breaking into a canter, and so making a false start. After considerable delay, the competitors known respectively by the names of "Pacific" and "Young America" made a fair start, the light buggies bounding after them at railway speed, their bold charioteers holding on by might and main. Pacific took the stakes, winning the first three out of five heats, and doing the first mile in 2 min. $22\frac{1}{2}$ secs., the second in 2 min. 26 secs., and the third in 2 min. 29 secs.

On our return from the race-course, in company with an American friend, we got from the subject of the turf to the sporting field. After listening for some time to his stories of gunning and hunting, or as we should simply term it shooting, he requested us in turn to give him a sketch of a day with the fox-hounds in the old country. Adverting to an English coloured print in an hotel at San Francisco, representing a "meet" with a good sprinkling of "pinks," he remarked, "I guess you chaps in the old country must have looked particular strange in those fixings," evidently believing that the traditional get-up of an English gentleman in the hunting field was quite obsolete. On our assuring him however this was very far from being the case, and that the pink, the buckskins, and the top-boots were still as much in vogue as ever, he was so much overcome with astonishment as to require to "liquor up" on the spot before continuing the conversation.

After describing the meet, the find, and the pack in full cry, during a twenty or thirty minutes' run, we went on to enlighten him as to the incidents that might possibly occur during a check, when our fox had run to cover, and how, after some delay, reynard would perhaps slink out again under the very noses of our horses.

We now endeavoured to make him understand the perfect silence that would be kept by the initiated until "Charley" had got a fair start, when, with a ringing "gone away! gone away!" we should settle ourselves in the saddle preparatory to another start, as soon as the hounds were again on the scent.

At this point in my narrative, my companion could contain himself no longer, but demanded, with mingled indignation and astonishment, to know how it was, after all our trial and trouble, that we allowed the fox to get off so easily, adding, "I would have blown his tarnation head off," thereby showing, to my great amusement, that up to that moment he had laboured under the strange delusion that every fox-hunter was fully armed with a double-barrelled fowling-piece. On assuring him that we carried no weapon more formidable than a hunting-whip, he was again so completely overcome, that he required to "liquor up" once more, ere he could sufficiently collect his scattered senses to appreciate the full extent of our folly.

While the operation of liquoring was going on before the bar, at a place lying about half-way between the race-course and the town, and which stood in the midst of pleasure-grounds, an acquaintance of our American friend happened to drop in, whom he accosted with "Well, General, how air you?" Our subsequent introduction to the General involved another general liquoring, as is universally the case on such occasions; and on our friend, in the course of conversation, giving the General a sketch of our account of an English fox-hunt, the latter guessed it must have been a "tall horse-back ride," but he evidently looked upon a fox as a very poor quarry. On his subsequently taking his departure, having been struck with the somewhat unsoldierlike appearance of the general, I asked our friend where he was quartered. He did not at first seem to understand the question, but eventually replied that he guessed he was located on Montgomery, meaning thereby that he lived in Montgomery Street. On proceeding to inquire what troops he was in command of, as we had not remarked any in or about San Francisco —this being during the period of our first visit, latterly we saw plenty of drilling and volunteers— he informed us that the General was no General at all, in the sense in which we had understood the term, but simply a "notary-general," this title being bestowed, indifferently, on any who have the right to affix the word "general" to their official designation, such as "attorney-general," "registrar-general," &c.

The habit of indulging in frequent drinking at public bars, or liquoring, as the Americans term it, is a national vice, which has already been commented on by other writers, and whose castigation I will leave to abler hands than mine, simply informing my readers that the bars are spacious and lofty, and often handsomely got up. They are of two classes, distinguished as "one bit" and "two bit" houses, a bit being either the eighth part of a dollar—a little more than sixpence—or a dime, the tenth part of the same sum, a less coin than which is never tendered in payment for anything ordered at a San Franciscan bar, copper coinage being quite unknown here. Lunch is always provided gratis to all customers, from about half-past twelve until half-past two. The bill of fare is, of course, not very varied, but the dishes are of good quality, especially in the "two bit" houses.

There are various places of amusement in San Francisco—the theatres, of which there are several, appearing to enjoy a special patronage. There is a good opera-house, at which operas are frequently very creditably performed.

A small club exists in San Francisco, called the "Union," and we must do the San Franciscans the justice to acknowledge that they display great readiness in electing strangers as members, during the period of their stay in the town, on the proposal of one member being backed by the recommendation of another—an act of courtesy which is also generally extended to the officers of the different European men-of-war in the harbour.

Great excitement was created during the period of our first stay at San Francisco, by the arrival of the "pony express" from St. Joseph's, or St. Joey, as it is more generally termed. No inconsiderable amount of interest had long been felt in the success of this undertaking, which aimed at establishing a direct communication for the transmission of telegrams* and letters across the American continent. This important and desirable object is sought to be accomplished by a chain of posts—at which relays of ponies are kept —from St. Joey, the last station on the railroad, communicating with New York and the Atlantic, to Sacramento and the Pacific. It will readily be understood that this service is one of considerable risk and hardship; the principal danger to which the messengers are exposed being the attacks of hostile Indians. The mail-bags are carried across the saddle, and the strap fastening them together

* A line of telegraph now exists all the way.

is so arranged under the rider, that the moment the man's weight is removed, in the event of his death, they must fall to the ground, and will then stand a chance of being found and recovered by the next messenger that follows in his traces.

Additional rejoicings occurred in consequence of the expeditious mode in which the transit had been effected, the distance from St. Joseph's to within fifty miles of Sacramento having been accomplished by the express in about eight days. Since then coaches have been established to run between San Francisco and St. Joseph's, which perform the journey in three weeks.

We cannot take leave of San Francisco without a passing notice of the Celestials, which singular people form no unimportant element in the floating population of the place. A considerable portion of the city is devoted wholly and exclusively to their use. The greater proportion are probably on their way to or from the different diggings and gold-fields, at the same time not a few are employed in various manual occupations in the docks, warehouses, and other waterside premises of this great emporium of the West. Finally, many among them have attained the position of wealthy merchants and traders, to which they have raised themselves by their own industry and perseverance.

The celebrated "Vigilance Committee," as it was called, of San Francisco, also deserves a few passing words of notice at our hands. Abuses of every description had, some years ago, assumed the most alarming proportions, and the rule of the mob had acquired an ascendancy such as threatened to be subversive of all the principles of law, order, and social life. The ballot boxes were tampered with to such an extent that men of the most infamous character were returned as members of the House of Representatives. Villains of the blackest dye sat on the magisterial bench, and the functions of officers of justice were performed by notorious thieves. Every law of decency and morality was openly violated, society in California appeared to be on the eve of dissolution, and the last barriers to the brutal passions and unbridled licentiousness of a mob of wretches, whose only law was the rule of "might is right," appeared about to be broken down.

Desperate evils require desperate remedies, and, to the honour of humanity be it said, men were found sufficiently brave and true-hearted to step forward at this frightful juncture, and organize a determined resistance to the progress of violence and licentiousness. Such was the origin of the famous "Vigilance Committee."

Of course I need hardly inform my readers that all their meetings were convened in the profoundest secrecy, and their whole plan of operation kept carefully concealed until all was ripe for execution.

So well were their measures taken, that on a particular day, fixed on beforehand, they issued forth in a body, well armed, and by a *coup de main* possessed themselves of the persons of some of the more notorious among the evil-doers—ringleaders in acts of iniquity—whose hands were freshly imbrued with the life-blood of their fellow-citizens. These wretches were brought to trial before a tribunal established by the committee, and condemned to punishments more or less severe. I believe only two of their number were actually hung. Thus, by the exercise of courage and determination, was the torrent of lawless violence arrested in its full course of destruction, and the principles of outraged justice once more openly vindicated. There can be no doubt that the political and social existence of California owes its salvation to the untiring efforts and exertions of the "Vigilance Committee."

Finding matters were going against them, many of the proscribed made their escape from California. I am much mistaken if I do not recognize the name of one of their number in an officer now holding a good position in the ranks of the Federal army.

## CHAPTER XV.

Departure from San Francisco—Benicia—Sacramento City—Its Situation—Natural Productions of California—Row in the House of Assembly—Use of the Revolver and Knife—Opinion of an American on American Institutions—Probable Effects of the Present War in the United States—Its Causes—Tariff to protect the Manufacturing Interests—Hatred between the North and South—Results to be anticipated at the Close of the War—Present Evils attending it—Necessity of taking Measures for the Protection of Canada—Bad Feeling shown by America towards England—Honourable Conduct of this Country—Defence of American Shores of the Lakes—The Canadian Militia—Speech of the Hon. John A. Macdonald at Quebec.

WE left San Francisco, or Frisco, as it is familiarly termed, for Sacramento, on board one of those huge floating hotels, or almost palaces, with which later descriptions and drawings have familiarized the English public. Suffice it therefore to say, the steamer in which we took our passage up the Sacramento River was a type of its class, having a cabin running its entire length, with a house for officers, a pilot house on deck fo'rard', and a drinking bar.

At the mouth of the Sacramento River is situated the foundry and factory of the Pacific Mail Steam Ship Company—by name Benicia—the place from which the doughty champion of the ring, Heenan, takes his well-known *sobriquet*. By what right the Americans lay claim to this powerfully built young giant, and boast him as a specimen of what their country can produce in the shape of muscular vigour and powers of endurance, we never could rightly understand. Both the parents of Heenan were natives of Ireland, and the mere accident of his having been born on the other side the Atlantic, cannot possibly be regarded as any criterion of the *physique* the American continent may be capable of producing.

On our way to Sacramento City, about one hundred miles up the river, we stopped at several places and took a quantity of fine fresh salmon on board. The town itself is situated on the left bank of the river, on very low ground, which is in parts exceedingly swampy, and liable to be flooded by an overflow of the waters of the river, a catastrophe that befell the place as recently as last winter; an account of which, together with views of the partially submerged town, appeared in the columns of the *Illustrated London News*.

Sacramento is a much smaller place than San

Francisco, but is the seat of Government and capital of California State. The House of Assembly and Senate meet in the principal building in the place called the Capitol, in which are also the law-courts. There are a great number of Chinese in this place, as in San Francisco.

The quality of the soil in this part of California is undoubtedly fine, and well adapted for all the purposes of agriculture. Great quantities of wheat are grown in the neighbourhood both of this place and San Francisco. Fruits and vegetables attain maturity much earlier in California than in the more northern latitude of British Columbia, and great quantities are exported to our colonies on this coast, as they can be brought up in a few days by the steamers. California may be regarded therefore as standing pretty much in the same relation to Vancouver and British Columbia that Portugal does to England.

During my stay in Sacramento one of those characteristic rows occurred in the House of Representatives for which America generally, and the Pacific States especially, have obtained such an unenviable notoriety. It arose out of some person in the gallery expressing aloud his approbation of the opinions to which one of the members was giving utterance. These on the other hand were as emphatically condemned by some one else, also one of the audience. This at once provoked an angry discussion, until, having applied to each other the opprobrious epithet of liar, one of the disputants drew forth his revolver and shot the other, stabbing him when he was down.

Such acts of lawless violence are unhappily only too common in America, and have come to be looked upon with comparative indifference, or at least as inevitable—men who have been guilty of what we should call murder in England being frequently acquitted by a jury of their countrymen, on the score of the provocation they had received. If the injury or insult be deemed sufficiently grave, Americans appear to think that a man is justified in wiping it out with blood whenever an opportunity may occur, even by an act of cold-blooded murder; for stabbing and shooting a man behind his back is unhappily of too frequent occurrence, and is by no means regarded with the loathing and execration such an act of dastardly villainy deserves. We have been horrified to hear Americans speak approvingly of deeds of violence perpetrated under circumstances that made an Englishman's blood boil with indignation, nor will they be brought to see the matter in its proper light. They will refuse to be convinced of the atrocious cowardice, as well as villainy, of shooting or stabbing a man behind his back without giving him a chance for his life, if they consider the original provocation to have been sufficiently great, and will reply, in answer to any remonstrance, "Serve him right, sir, serve him right, shoot him like a dog!"

The habit of carrying sheath knives, and even revolvers in the pockets, so common in America, and especially in these countries of the Far West, cannot be too strongly reprobated, as the fact of always having a deadly weapon close at hand often leads to the fatal termination of what would otherwise end as an ordinary dispute.

Before I left California last year a meeting was convened by those favourable to Southern interests to discuss the rights, the justice of the cause, and the future prospects of the then recently seceded States. Before opening proceedings it was unanimously agreed that the discussion should be carried on in the most perfectly friendly and impartial manner, and that speakers who might profess Union sentiments should be allowed to state them as freely and as fully as those of Southern proclivities. Alas! for these good intentions! The assembly soon waxed noisy and disputatious, argument degenerated into recrimination, and the opposite parties were on the point of proceeding to back their opinions by the bullet and the bowie-knife. Several revolvers had actually been produced, when some one possessing more discretion, if not more valour, than the rest, bethought himself of the happy expedient of turning off the gas. By thus putting a sudden stop to the proceedings, and plunging the entire assembly into total darkness, a disgraceful scene of riot and bloodshed was in all probability prevented.

The notoriously boastful disposition of Americans generally has already been sufficiently often commented on by all writers on this people; I shall not therefore trouble the reader by relating how often I was compelled to listen, *ad nauseam*, to windy arguments that were intended to prove that America was not only the most favoured by nature of all regions under the sun, but that all her institutions, political and social, were such as might well excite the envy of every other nation. Recent events must surely by this time have opened their eyes to some of their weak points, and convinced them that perfection is as difficult of attainment on their own side the Atlantic as on this. The wild buffeting of wind and wave to which the model Republic is at present subjected must, by this time, have discovered many a rotten plank and loose screw in the vessel of the State. Let us hope that they will so far profit by their present experience as to learn at least a lesson of humility. In justice, however, to the penetration and common sense of the Americans, I must state that I am fully convinced that many among them, even while professing to participate in a senseless admiration of all their customs and institutions, hold at heart very different opinions.

I will, in conclusion, repeat a few observations let fall by a friend of mine in San Francisco, who was himself from one of the Eastern States, and strongly in favour of the Union. "Our liberty, equality, and fraternity, sir," he would say, "are all moonshine, our boasted freedom is a snare and a delusion. My countrymen want to travel more, to correct their intolerable vanity and self-sufficiency. I have travelled a great deal, and have come to see that there are a vast number of shams and abuses tolerated in this country whose existence I might perhaps never have suspected if I had not had the opportunity of becoming acquainted with the political institutions of other countries. Talk of universal equality—universal humbug! sir," he would say, "no, no; there is less of the genuine article to be found in this very State of California than in any other country under the sun. The fact is that a man with money, friends, and interest to back him, may do almost anything, even to committing manslaughter, with impunity. The influence of money is paramount; wealth is but another name for political power, social position, and even judicial immunity. Our magisterial bench is not free from the taint of venality, and our trials are too often disgraceful mockeries, both judge and jury having previously made up their minds as to the verdict to be given. The despotism with which we are cursed, sir, is the despotism of the dollar, and a grinding, degrading despotism it is. You may depend upon it," he added, "I shall not remain a day longer in the place than I can help,"—alluding, of course, to California. The reader will understand that I do not offer these remarks as the result of my own observation and experience, but give them just as I received them from the lips of a born American.

Lest I should be thought, however, to have borne rather hardly on American manners and customs, I am prepared to acknowledge that I have known many Americans who were not only men of enlightened and liberal views, but gentlemen in every sense of the term.

The terrible struggle now raging between the North and South, or, as they call themselves, the "Federals and Confederates" of the formerly United States, must exercise so important an influence on the future, not only of this people, but on that of all other races inhabiting the American continent, that it may well claim a few passing observations at our hands.

Into the question of the justice of the present war I will not pause to inquire. The British public has already listened to sufficient arguments in favour of Secession on the one hand, and vindicating the course taken by the Federal Government on the other.

From all I know of America and its inhabitants,

I am convinced that the causes that have led to the present outbreak are various and of long standing; that their germs have in fact existed from the moment the great Republic was established, and have gone on increasing and developing ever since, and gradually undermining the political cohesion and integrity of the Federal Republic, that boasted itself the model of such institutions and the envy of the universe. Ever since the very foundation of the State, after the War of Independence, elements of discord have existed between the Northern and Southern portions of the Republic, such as must, in the opinion of all enlightened Americans with whom I have discussed the question, have eventually produced the present rupture.

The question of slavery is but an accidental circumstance, surrounded by a host of other clashing interests, complicating the situation indeed, but not in itself the real cause of difference. I feel assured that, had the institution of slavery never existed on the American soil, there are sufficient other causes for the present war, both political, geographical, and social. One of the chief elements of weakness may be traced to the want of cohesion among the different States of the Union, and the absence of any powerful centralizing influence. Each State possesses an independent political organization, an Executive of its own, and aims at a separate and individual existence. Devoted exclusively to the pursuit of its own interests, even to the prejudice of those of the community at large, each State is ambitious of leading, and a spirit of rivalry, dangerous to the political integrity of the Federal Republic, is, as a natural consequence, engendered.

Again, the system of taxation, levied exclusively for the benefit of the North Eastern States of the Union on all foreign produce, has long been a source of bitter heart-burning and recrimination on the part of their Southern and Western fellow-citizens, who are forced to pay a high duty on all imported articles, exclusively to fill the pockets of the Northern manufacturers.

The Southern States, not unreasonably, object to pay a higher price for every article they receive from abroad than what they could obtain it for direct through their own ports.

A great proportion of the electors of the Northern and Eastern States are either manufacturers themselves, or in the manufacturing interest, and being unable to compete with European manufacturers, have established a high protective tariff for their own especial benefit, to the detriment of the community at large.*

* The Tariff recently presented by Mr. Stevens to the House of Representatives would seem to indicate that this infatuated people are prepared to go to even greater lengths in the matter of protection, and to pursue the suicidal policy of cutting themselves off from the commerce of the universe for the sake of venting their spleen on England and France.

Independently of all causes of political difference, I am convinced that there has long existed a deep-rooted natural antipathy between the North and South. This hatred, bitter and rancorous as one of race and creed, it would perhaps be difficult to trace to its origin; that the events of the last few years have served to foster and develop it will be readily understood. Whatever be the cause of it, there can be no doubt that the contempt and execration in which the "Yankee" is held by all classes "down South," is such as no description of mine would enable any one who has never been in the country, to realize.

That the Southern planters and landowners, many of them men of good family and breeding—scions not unfrequently of an old and honourable stock in the United Kingdom—should object to bow their necks to be trampled on by the roughshod mobocracy of New York, is not to be wondered at. A democracy may be a very good thing in its way, if only carried out in the spirit in which such a form of Government was originally framed; but, of all Governments under the sun, a mobocracy is the most odious and intolerable.

From all I saw and heard during my stay in America, especially in the Eastern States, in the autumn of last year, I never doubted that the present dissolution of the Union was final. Whatever be the future political organization of this vast region, there can be no doubt that the North and South will still be sufficiently powerful, sufficiently large, and sufficiently favoured by nature, in the varied productions of their soil, to maintain a separate and individual political existence. Each will still possess, for ages to come, a vast outlet for its surplus population. What is to be regretted is, not so much the dissolution of the Union, as the present frightful fratricidal war, the effect of which must not only be to throw back the material progress of the United States some half century, to burden a young country with the incubus of a national debt and a greatly increased taxation, but must, inevitably, leave behind it fatal memories of deeds of violence and blood, that it will take ages to efface. Let us hope that, as there is no evil without its concomitant good, the American character may, in passing through the present terrible ordeal, be purged, as by fire, of many of its faults and imperfections, and that both parties may awake from their frenzied dream of conquest and bloodshed, not only wiser but better men.

Whatever be the issue of the present conflict, its results must be fraught with importance to the whole North American continent. The preponderating political influence of the United States will be divided among the other countries and States forming portions of it. There can be no doubt that many will be driven by the present war from the United States, to seek, under British rule, for that stable and secure government which the latter country, in its present disorganized state, cannot be expected to afford. Capitalists settled in New York and the other great centres of American commerce, will naturally be disposed, especially if they be of English origin, to transfer their fortunes and persons across the Canadian frontier.

At a moment when it appears possible that the future government of the United States may be a military despotism, with an immense armed force at its disposal, it is natural that we should feel, if not anxiety, at least some solicitude with regard to the future of Canada. It may be argued that, on issuing from her present struggle, the United States will hardly be justified, on financial grounds, in engaging in another war; nor am I myself disposed to regard the ravings and empty braggadocio of the New York press as the expression of the opinion and feelings of the better classes in America towards England, but we must remember that a mob acts without reflection, and on the impulse of the moment. In any case, it is right to be prepared, even while refusing to admit that there is any just cause for alarm. The ill feeling manifested by the Federals towards England, from the commencement of the present war, I regard as wholly irrational and unjustifiable. I consider the line of conduct pursued by this country towards both contending parties, as having been in the highest degree honourable and impartial. To the serious injury of our own manufacturing interests, have we steadily adhered to our avowed policy of perfect neutrality. Our Government has constantly refused to become a party to any act of intervention, even in concert with our ally, the Emperor of the French. I would ask our American friends whether they think that any other Power, say France or Russia, would not have availed itself of the present opportunity of asserting its dominion over the Island of St. Juan, to which the Americans put forth such an unfounded claim, and one so arrogantly maintained, and which is still unsettled. We have not only abstained from attempting to gain any advantage, but have generously submitted to great inconvenience and loss, rather than give them any cause of complaint. Under these circumstances, I must confess to feeling somewhat indignant at the equally contemptible and irrational ill-will that the Federals have constantly displayed towards England. Let us hope that their eyes may be opened to see matters in their true light, and to recognize rather the claims that this country has on their gratitude than to take up a party cry of senseless vituperation.

I see that the subject of the defences of the great chain of lakes separating British America from the United States, has quite recently been brought before the Executive of the latter country, at a meeting of the New York delegation in Congress. The principal topics discussed were the present undefended condition of the lakes, and the great extent and rapid growth of commerce on their waters. The principal measures that are likely to arise out of these discussions, to occupy the attention of Congress, will be the opening of adequate channels of water communication from the eastern and western extremities of the lakes; the first to be affected by enlarging the locks on the Erie and Oswego canals and the other by the enlargement of the canal from the Chicago and Illinois River: thus permitting the passage of vessels of war, in the shape of gun-boats, for the defence of these internal waters.*

Taking all these circumstances into consideration, and bearing in mind that, whatever the issue of the present internecine war, the United States can never be without a standing army, I think that the fact of our having so powerful an armed neighbour on our frontier, must entail on us the necessity of maintaining an armed force also in Canada, or, at least, such a one as shall serve as the nucleus of a larger body. This nucleus ought, in my opinion, to be furnished by the active force of Canadian Militia. In connection with this important subject I will take the liberty of making the following

* Since this was written, the *Times* has drawn public attention to the same subject.

extracts from the speech of the Honourable John A. Macdonald, the Attorney-General for Canada, delivered in the Legislative Assembly, Quebec, during last May, without subscribing, however, to all the opinions he expressed:—

"There is one point with regard to which I confess I am exceedingly dissatisfied, and I would implore the honourable gentlemen who compose the Administration of the day, to pause and reconsider their resolve to defer anything like a preparation for the defence of the country for another year. The very idea makes me stand aghast, that this country (Canada) is to stand defenceless till mid-winter, till—no matter what the exigency or danger may be, no matter what the relations between England and the United States—though every exposed inch of our frontier may be covered by hostile American riflemen, we shall have no means of communication with England — when — however strongly England may be aroused to send assistance to her liege subjects in danger—we shall have no means of communication, and no means of defending ourselves—without arms, without organization, without a militia force.

"I cannot conceal from myself that we are now, in Canada, in a more dangerous position than we have ever been before, since the period immediately preceding the surrender of the Southern Ambassadors. What does every mail now bring us from

England? Do we not receive accounts that many of the industrial population, both of England and France, are in a state of starvation; that thousands, almost millions, are being left without the means of subsistence, in consequence of this most disastrous war; that in France more than in England the pressure is great, increasing and imminent, so that the arrival of every mail gives increasing reason to apprehend a forced intervention? And if intervention is forced upon the Emperor of France by the starving population of that country, do we not know that England also of necessity will be dragged into it? And then what will be the consequence? The Americans have declared that the first sign of intervention by France or England, will be a signal for war.

"I am happy to find that the present Administration admit the necessity of a militia organization, and that it forms a portion of their policy. But if we want a Militia Bill at all, we want it now. We want arms in our hands and arms in our armories. We want them now. Next winter it may be too late. God forbid that such an event should happen, but I would ask my honourable friends, the members of this Administration, to consider the danger we incur should any hostile feeling unhappily arise between England and the United States between now and next winter. In such an event, their names would go down to posterity as having betrayed the best interests of their country for the mere convenience of their own governmental arrangements; as having, for this, run the risk of our rights, our liberties, and our existence as a people being swept away. For the want of this necessary preparation, we may be whipped in—as the Northern States are now endeavouring to whip in the South—may be whipped into a position of dependence on the people of the American Union, as was the fate of that poor remnant of Mexicans who, by force of arms, were made the slaves of that Union.

"While I give every member credit for the vote he gave on the Militia Bill, I know what will be the feeling in England when the news of the fate of that measure arrives there. The people of England will not be able to understand the motives which induced gentlemen to vote against the second reading, and therefore, as will of course be inferred, against the principle of the bill. They will say, we were willing to help Canada to carry out the pledge given by the British nation that the whole power of the empire would be exerted in our behalf in case of foreign invasion; but what can we think of men who will not even consider the principle of a measure to enable them to fight for their own liberties, their own soil, their own country? I have no hesitation in expressing my belief that the moment that news arrives in England, our securities will fall in value, and the influence and standing of Canada will be most seriously shaken.

"Not only will the rejection of the Militia Bill have the effect I have stated in England, but it will be taken in the Northern States as an encouragement of the idea that Canada is ripe for annexation. It will encourage the United States to attack us, and will discourage England from coming to our aid. Yet here we are, while this continent is in so disturbed a state—while Canada is in danger—here we are folding our hands, and saying we will be ready to prepare to fight nine months hence. Now is the time for organization, and that man would be a traitor to the best interests of his country, who would not urge by argument and by vote, and by every means in his power, the necessity of immediate armament to defend our country and ourselves. That is the first and most important of the considerations which I would press upon the gentlemen supporting the Administration why there should only be an adjournment long enough to enable the members of the Government to be re-elected. I hope the election of none of them will be opposed.

"There is another subject to which I have no doubt that during the short period my honourable friends have been in the Administration their attention has been called, and that is the great importance that, before this Parliament prorogues, the question of the International Railroad should be taken up. I have reason to believe, and I dare say my honourable friends in the Government, from their official position, know that the Imperial Government are now prepared to meet us half way for the construction of that road, that they are ready to borrow on their own credit, and at a low rate of interest which their credit will secure, the whole amount of money necessary to construct the Intercolonial Railroad, receiving in exchange the security of the several colonies. I believe that if that is carried out Canada will be making a much better bargain than that originally proposed.

"But we do not know how long that may last. We know that the able man at the head of the British Government is old and frail, and the moment the keystone of the arch is swept away by any accident, his whole Administration will fall with him, and a new Administration will come in, altogether unbound by this proposition or anything like it. We may lose by delay for ever the chance of an Intercolonial Railroad, and may lose with it for a long period the chance of having a Pacific Railroad, which would be the eventual sequence of an Intercolonial Railroad extending from Halifax to our Western Lakes. All this may be lost by our prorogation, because the Government cannot act without provincial legislation.

"I might point out other reasons, but these may suffice, and I hope the honourable gentlemen who compose the Administration will reconsider the matter. I feel strongly on these two points—our railway interests, which will remain involved till we have railroad legislation and the Intercolonial Railroad finished, and the necessity, above all else, of some legislation that will save the province from being left till next winter bound hand and foot, unarmed, helpless, and without the means of defence. But I implore them again—I ask them as Canadians, as men whose reputation may be for ever lost if a single shot should be fired, or a single foreign soldier advanced on our frontier, whether they will not stand inculpated, if such a thing should happen, as having in a time of great hazard been faithless to the best interests of their country?"

The recent debate on the defence of Canada, in the House of Lords, has again drawn public attention to this important question. It is gratifying to find that the speech of his Excellency Governor-General Monck, at Montreal, was received in the best possible spirit, and I think we may venture to hope that the well-known loyalty of this important colony may assume the practical form of a sufficiently numerous and well-armed militia to render it, comparatively speaking, independent of the assistance of the mother country.

## CHAPTER XVI.

General Remarks on the Origin and Present Condition of the Colonies of British Columbia and Vancouver's Island—Influence of the Gold Discovery—Neglect of many Important Branches of Industry—Discovery of Copper Mines—Prospects of Immigrants—State of Industry—High Rate of Wages—Inconvenience caused by a Former Want of a Circulating Medium—Despatch of Governor Douglas—Establishment of a Mint and Assay Office—Banks in Victoria—Import Duty and Tariffs in British Columbia—Protection claimed by the Farmers of Vancouver's Island—The Charter of the Hudson's Bay Company—Debate in the House of Lords on the Subject—Speech of the Duke of Newcastle.

THE rapid growth of the colonies of British Columbia and Vancouver's Island, the energy displayed in opening up routes into the interior, the sudden influx of population, the startling way in which towns have sprung up in the midst of the pine-covered wilderness, and isolated Hudson's Bay Forts expanded into flourishing settlements, will ever be remarkable among the achievements of our age. At the same time, this very rapidity of growth has developed certain principles of internal policy and legislation, to the exclusion of others of perhaps equal or greater importance. The discovery of gold has imparted a stimulus and energy to certain special branches of industry, to the prejudice or neglect of others of possibly more vital importance to the real interests of a new colony. Doubtless these are merely temporary evils, inseparable from a state of things so extraordinary and abnormal as attended the birth and early growth of British Columbia and Vancouver's Island. At the same time I think it right to advert to one or two points of domestic policy and industry which have perhaps been overlooked or neglected in the excitement caused by the discovery of gold, and at the same time partially to indicate what, in my humble opinion, will be the safest course to be pursued with a view to the future prosperity and well-being of these interesting colonies.

British Columbia, at the era of her gold discoveries, differed from both Australia and California. She was nothing but a pathless wilderness when the gold excitement commenced in 1858. Round a few of the scattered forts of the Hudson's Bay Company there were isolated patches of cultivation, but the amount of labour devoted to the culture of the soil was wholly unimportant. The white men, equally with the Indian tribes inhabiting the country, may virtually be said to have subsisted on the produce of the chase. With the influx of immigrants came an increased demand for supplies of food, and as nothing but fish or game could be had, of necessity, with these exceptions, every article of food had to be brought from abroad. The search for gold occupied industry so exclusively that but very few persons found time to engage in agriculture. As a natural consequence, a large proportion of the gains of the colony went to enrich the foreign agriculturists who supplied its inhabitants with the necessary articles of food. Thus the mineral wealth of British Columbia became in the end beneficial rather to her neighbours than to herself. I am aware that this is a matter to which I have already drawn the reader's attention, but I regard it as one of such paramount importance, in connection with the future prospects of the colony, that I venture to extract the following remarks on the subject from the *Victoria British Colonist*:—

"The town and country begin to swarm with men; most of them are inured to labour. The majority, perhaps, are better acquainted with agriculture than with any other art. Yet all profess to be bound for Cariboo. Agriculture seems never to be taken into account. Elsewhere the agricultural labourer has been so poorly paid that there seems to be a prevailing idea that agriculture can never pay as well as gold-digging. We regard this as a popular error. It is a fallacy—a perfect fallacy so far as British Columbia is concerned. We are persuaded that by digging no deeper than six inches from the surface the farmer may realize as handsome a return in gold as the miner who delves in the creeks of Cariboo. We may find it extremely difficult to persuade those who are most competent to engage in it that such is really the case; yet it is none the less true. It is not only true that a farmer on the route from Lytton and Lillooett to William's Lake, Alexandria, the mouth of Quesnelle or Swift River, can be rewarded for his labour, but there is a positive certainty that he will be well paid into the bargain. Were there such a thing as a positive certainty that every miner who would go to Cariboo would be successful, make his pile of one, five, ten, or 20,000 dollars, it might be useless with our present population to recommend farming. But there is no such thing as a certainty of making a fortune in gold mines anywhere, whether in Cariboo, Salmon River, California, or Australia. In all gold-diggings there are a great many blanks, and few prizes; and although we are persuaded that Cariboo is fabulously rich in gold, yet we have no idea that the majority who may go there this year can return with a fortune. We want, then, to impress upon some of our readers that there is one way in which a fortune can be made in British Columbia without breasting the snow on the Bald Hills, or packing beans and bacon on their back from creek to creek in Cariboo. That way is simply by taking up farms on the road to Cariboo. That way is by raising hay, oats, wheat, barley, potatoes, beans, pork, beef, and mutton. These are the commodities that can be most easily exchanged for gold. One hundred and sixty acres of good land anywhere from Bonaparte River to the mouth of the Quesnelle will, on the average, prove a far better claim than the average of claims in the mines. Such, would be a claim that can be worked every year for the next century, and within the next five years make any industrious man's fortune. There is not a country under the fair face of heaven that now offers such brilliant inducements to the farmer as British Columbia. The climate is healthy and invigorating, the soil fertile and yields abundantly, and a market at starvation prices at every farmer's door.

"Foreign produce can never compete; or only so long as the domestic supply is inadequate to the demand. At the present moment the supply of farm produce consumed, or to be consumed this year in the mines, has to be brought from Oregon or California. It has to be carried from 500 to 1,000 miles before it is landed in British Columbia, and then it traverses the country from 200 to 400 miles before it reaches the consumer; and, what is still more worthy of notice, before it can be brought into competition with those who may take up a *ranch\** anywhere on the road to Cariboo.

"If a farmer in any other country could only save the cost of transportation on produce between San Francisco, or Portland, and Lillooett, and Lytton, he would enjoy an unequalled market. But besides the cost of freight, the farmer in the sister colony has the protection of ten per cent. duty. Over all, he can get a high price for whatever he may raise, and sell it at his door. Let any one who understands farming, make a calculation of what it will cost to live and grow a crop on the Cariboo road this year; then deduct the cost from the probable value of his crop, and he will be convinced that farming in British Columbia is no second-class business.

"Were farms taken up along the new lines of road from Lillooett and Lytton to Williams' Lake and Alexandria, every pound of hay and barley that can be raised this year would find a market. For next winter we expect to chronicle the transportation of merchandise on sleds to Alexandria, and other points in the direction of the mines. The animals engaged on the route will consume

---

\* A settlement, whether white or red.

all the fodder; and this time next year we anticipate chronicling such a supply of provisions in the upper country, carried there over the snow, as will render it unnecessary to move any more in that direction till the trails become perfectly good. The quantity of merchandise will, no doubt, be very great, for whatever the mining population may need this year, it will certainly be far greater next spring. Let every farmer then take into account the quantity of fodder required, and the amount of agricultural produce necessary for the mines, and he will discover a veritable Pactolus in the stream of immigrants running winter and summer to and from Cariboo. Let farmers also recollect that those who take up farms early on the route, will have an excellent chance to add to their finances by keeping wayside inns, providing ' accommodation for man and beast.' "

I regret to find that since I adverted to the probability of a scarcity of provisions at the diggings my prognostications have been fully verified. According to the latest advices from British Columbia, not a single pack-train had left Lillooett up to the 2nd of May, owing to the bad state of the roads, resulting from the late severe winter. The total want of all the necessaries of life had compelled many miners to return from the gold districts. I entertain no doubt, however, that this evil has long since been remedied.

Fresh discoveries are daily bringing to light the fact that the Colonies of British Columbia and Vancouver's Island, with their dependencies, are rich not only in gold, but also in silver, copper, iron, lead, tin, coal, &c. Recent accounts would seem to indicate that copper mining will, ere long, become an important branch of industry in both colonies. Indications of copper are everywhere found in the extensive Archipelago that commences at the entrance of the Gulf of Georgia, and stretches northward to the islands that skirt Russian America. It will no doubt take ages fully to explore the mineral wealth of the coast of British Columbia. One especial advantage to be derived from these mines would be the fact of their affording winter employment to the gold miners, the want of which has long been felt to be a serious drawback to the industry of the colony. In the absence of winter diggings—tunnel-diggings—that can be worked longer than those of Cariboo, that is to say, during five or six months in the year only, the copper mines of the coast become doubly important and valuable. They would not only provide employment to numbers all the year round, but might, I think, prove a profitable market for labour after the gold-mining season had closed.

It is no doubt unnecessary to inform my readers that in the colonies of British Columbia and Vancouver's Island, as elsewhere, the Crown owns all the mines, whether of the precious metals—gold and silver—or of copper, and other base metals, except where it has conveyed away its right to the precious metals by a grant or lease, or to the base metals by pre-emption or purchase. The right of the Crown to the precious metals is reserved from pre-emption, but no reservation is made of the base metals; thus, to become the owner of copper, lead, iron, tin, or coal mines in either colony, all that is required is to purchase the land; or if the land be Crown land, any British subject, or alien who may take the oath of allegiance, may pre-empt the land in which these minerals are found, and by complying with the conditions of the "Pre-emption Consolidation Act" of British Columbia, or the "Pre-emption Act" of Vancouver's Island, as the case may be, he can become absolute owner of the land and the base minerals which it contains.

Without specifying the various branches of industry in which he might engage, the number and extent of which must be apparent from the tenor of my foregoing remarks, I may state in general terms, that these colonies offer the greatest possible inducements to the capitalist. As a rule, the newer the colony the higher the rate of interest, and the more numerous the openings for investments. Money in Victoria can be lent on good security, at rates ranging from twenty-five to thirty per cent. All skilled artizans may feel sure of commanding a very high rate of wages, and cannot fail to do well; and, finally, female servants are at premium. What a pity it is some thousands of the young needlewomen and others in London, who find it so hard, with all their toil and drudgery, to earn a precarious subsistence, cannot be transported to the shores of our El Dorado of the West. I submit the idea for the consideration of those whose philanthropy and wealth might induce them to carry it into execution.

The following remarks of the Governor, Mr. Douglas, in a despatch to the Colonial Secretary, dated November, 1861, point out the existence of a want which has long been felt to be a serious bar to the commercial prosperity of the colony :—

"Much inconvenience and loss have, ever since the formation of these colonies, been occasioned by the want of a circulating medium of fixed and recognized value, equal to the business demands of the country. The scarcity of coin has been so great, gold-dust not being received for duties, that importers of goods have found it difficult at all times to make their custom-house payments, and, as is well known, are frequently compelled to borrow money for that purpose, at exorbitant rates of interest, from two per cent. per month, and upwards. Almost all the business of the country is transacted in gold-dust of uncertain value, and it is easy to conceive the difficulty and inconvenience of adjusting payments by such means, when the holder and receiver are both alike subject to loss, and fearful of imposition."

"The effects of an over-restricted monetary circulation are now, however, operating so fatally in both colonies, that it is indespensable to provide a remedy for an evil that is sapping the very foundations of our prosperity. To illustrate this fact, I would inform your Grace that at this moment there is an amount of gold dust in the hands of miners from Cariboo, residing at Victoria, exceeding one quarter of a million sterling, and so great is the present dearth of coin that it brings a premium of five per cent. and over when procurable, which is not generally the case, as men may be seen hawking bars of gold about the streets of Victoria who cannot raise coin enough, even at the high rates of discount just mentioned, to defray their current expenses.

"The miners and other holders of gold are naturally incensed, and refuse to submit to this depreciation on the value of their property when they know it can be converted into coin for the moderate charge of one half of one per cent. at the United States Branch Mint in San Francisco, making an important saving to them of four and a half per cent. They are consequently leaving Victoria by every opportunity, and it is most painful to witness a state of things which is rapidly driving population and capital from the country.

"As a safer remedy, and one more suitable to the actual circumstances of the colonies, I propose to take immediate steps for the manufacture of gold pieces equal in value to the ten and twenty dollar American coins, and to bring them into general use, as a circulating medium in both colonies.

"This plan does not contemplate refining the gold, as the expense would be greatly increased by that process; it is merely proposed to bring it to a uniform standard of fineness, without separating the natural alloy of silver, which to some extent exists in all the gold of British Columbia.

"The pieces will be prepared at the Government Assay Office, and will bear the stamp of unquestionable character; and I am of opinion that by making the gold contained in them of the full current value of the piece, without taking the silver into account, which I propose should go as a bonus they will not only answer as a cheap and convenient currency within the colonies, but also have the same exchange value when exported to other countries."

Since this was written, I am aware that steps have been taken to carry out the idea of Mr. Douglas. Mr. F. Claudet, of the Assay Office, New Westminster, spent a portion of the winter in California, engaged in procuring the necessary machinery for establishing a Mint in British Columbia. I entertain therefore little doubt that by this time the gold pieces above referred to are in actual circulation.

I have recently noticed that a new company has been advertised, and probably by this time organized to carry on banking business in British Columbia and Vancouver's Island, where branch offices of the British Columbia and Vancouver's Island Banking and Gold Trading Company are to be established. Whether the concern is likely to prove remunerative to its originators and shareholders, time alone can determine. I might, however, remark that several well-established banking houses exist in Victoria, Vancouver's Island, doing trade with the interior of British Columbia, two of the most important of which are the Victoria Branch of the Bank of British North America, whose head office in London is 7, St. Helen's Place, Bishopsgate Street, and the branch office of the firm of Wells, Fargo & Co., both situated in Yates Street, the principal street in Victoria.

The executive of Vancouver consists of a Governor, a Council, and a House of Representatives, chosen from the different towns and districts into which the colony is divided. Victoria, its present capital and seat of Government, enjoys the additional privilege and advantage of being the chief emporium for the trade, not only of this colony, but also of British Columbia. This is to be attributed to the fact of its being a free port; whereas, every article of merchandise introduced into British Columbia is subject to an import duty—the tariff being decidedly high, in addition to which, every individual landing in this colony has to pay a polltax of one dollar per head. Now, although I do not for one moment pretend to question the wisdom of the policy that has led to the imposition of these tolls, yet I must confess that it does seem to me that they are levied too indiscriminately, and without a due regard to the true interests of the colony.

Be this as it may, there can be no doubt that the proximity of a free port like Victoria operates prejudicially on New Westminster, the capital of British Columbia. At the former place, for instance, a ship might be built at little more than the cost price value—exclusive of labour—of every article employed in its construction, whereas at New Westminster an import duty would have to be paid on every sheet of copper on its bottom.

On the other hand, the farmers of Vancouver cry out for Government protection, as agriculture, being here still somewhat in its infancy, they find it impossible to compete with the wealthy and extensive farmers of Oregon, a territory that has now been under cultivation for many years. At the present moment we believe that cereals can be introduced into the Port of Victoria at as cheap a rate as they can be produced in the colony of Vancouver. The cattle also, supplied for the use of the Royal Navy, come almost entirely from the United States territory of Oregon. As the resources of our own colonies are more fully developed, however, I entertain no doubt that they will be able to compete successfully with their neighbours.

Writing on the subject of the prospect for farmers emigrating to British Columbia, the *Victoria Press* says that:—

"The matter of supplying this colony with stock of all kinds is every day assuming more important proportions. During the past year our Customs' returns show that 7,031 head of live stock, to the value of 313,797 dollars, were imported by us; and as live stock only is liable to duty, dead carcases being admitted free, a large portion of what was consumed here was brought in dead, and consequently does not appear in the above returns; the value of which might be set down at 25,000 dollars, making the total for the year 338,597 dollars. When we remember that the greater part of this stock is brought from Oregon, and that this colony is at least its equal for purposes of grazing, it is a matter of surprise that we should be content to depend upon a foreign neighbour for a supply of that which we can very well produce at home at a lower price and with great advantage to the colony."

I cannot take leave of my subject without a passing allusion to the question of the indemnity claimed by the Hudson's Bay Company for the vast possessions lying between Canada and the Rocky Mountains, which they hold in virtue of a Royal Charter granted to this company in the reign of Charles II. The territory conveyed to them, in fee simple, comprises the whole of the fertile districts of Central America, on the Red River and the Saskatchewan, as well as the auriferous regions—if any be found to exist—on the eastern slope of the Rocky Mountains, a tract of country which, in point of extent and natural resources, as also on account of its future prospects, might well excite the envy of many a potentate.

In connection with this important question, therefore, I venture to make the following extract from the able speech made by the Duke of Newcastle in the House of Lords on the evening of the 4th of July last:—

"The claim of the Hudson's Bay Company was to an entire fee simple in the soil over a district so vast, that at the rate of only 1d. per acre it would cost 700,000*l.* The company said that if the Government took the Saskatchewan from them it ought to buy them out entirely; and they spoke of a million and a half sterling as the price they would require for the surrender of their rights.

"Of course it would be impossible to ask the

House of Commons for any such sum for any such purpose. He doubted whether the company's charter ever was legal, but he was sensible how dangerous it would be to attempt to set it aside after it had been in existence 200 years. He did not deny that a necessity might arise for doing so, but he did not think that he was at present called upon to propose so strong a measure. He could not help hoping that some arrangement might be come to. At present he did not see his way, but he assured the noble lord and the house that he thought it a matter of paramount importance, and that he should not lose any opportunity of arranging with the company, if it were possible to do so. He would not undertake to offer either the large sum he had mentioned, or any other large sum to the company, as he thought it was out of the question that any large sum should be paid to them. The company could no more prevent men from settling in that district than they could prevent men from sailing on the ocean. He had no objection to lay the correspondence on the table of the House. He could only hope that by further negotiation some satisfactory progress would shortly be made towards coming to an arrangement, and he thought that the company should give facilities for a full postal and telegraphic communication between Halifax on the one hand and New Westminster on the other."

In allusion to the question of overland routes to British Columbia, the Duke also makes the following interesting remarks :—

" He thought it would be possible also for an expenditure of 100,000*l.* to form a communication through Canada, and he believed that the journey might be brought within thirty days. He thought that the colony itself might be properly called upon to contribute to the expense, and also that Canada would not only provide the roads within its own territory, but would likewise assist in extending the line towards British Columbia."

While fully acknowledging the justice of the observations made by the noble Duke on the subject of the monopoly possessed by the Hudson's Bay Company, and, at the same time, expressing my hope that the question may meet with a speedy and satisfactory settlement, I can heartily endorse the following remarks at the conclusion of a leader in the *Morning Post* of the 5th of July, which, in fact, but embody a similar tribute to the various good qualities of the Hudson's Bay traders, paid them by Lord Taunton in his speech on the preceding evening :—

" Although we cannot look with favour on a company which possesses so gigantic a monopoly, and are lords of so vast a territory, still we must do them justice where justice is due. They have been the sovereign rulers for two centuries over a territory peopled solely by the red man. They have exercised their sway with humanity, forbearance, and moderation. To their eternal credit be it spoken, they have neither brutalized nor exterminated the tribes of Indians which inhabit their hunting grounds. Without on any single occasion calling on the aid of the Government, they have succeeded in maintaining tranquillity, and enforcing respect for human life, amongst the wilds of the Far West. For having pursued this policy they have already earned the gratitude of the aborigines, and are not less entitled to the favourable consideration of the British nation."

# APPENDIX.

# APPENDIX.

## I.

RULES AND REGULATIONS FOR THE WORKING OF GOLD MINES, ISSUED IN CONFORMITY WITH THE GOLD FIELDS ACT, 1859.

WHEREAS it is provided by the Gold Fields Act, 1859, that the Governor, for the time being, of British Columbia, may, by writing under his hand and the public seal of the colony, make rules and regulations in the nature of by-laws for all matters relating to mining.

And whereas, in conformity with the said Act, certain rules and regulations have already been issued bearing date the 7th of September, 1859.

1. The mines in the said level benches shall be known as "bench diggings," and shall, for the purpose of ascertaining the size of claims therein, be

excepted out of the class of "dry diggings," as defined in the rules and regulations of the 7th of September last.

2. The ordinary claims on any bench diggings shall be registered by the gold commissioner according to such one of the two following methods of measurement as he shall deem most advantageous on each mine, viz.: One hundred feet square, or else a strip of land twenty-five feet deep at the edge of the cliff next the river, and bounded by two straight lines carried as nearly as possible, in each case, perpendicular to the general direction of such cliff across the level bench up to, and not beyond the foot of the descent in the rear; and in such last mentioned case, the space included between such two boundary lines when produced over the face of the cliff in front as far as the foot of such cliff and no farther, and all mines in the space so included shall also form a part of such claim.

3. The gold commissioner shall have authority in cases where the benches are narrow, to mark the claims in such manner as he shall think fit, so as to include an adequate claim. And shall also

have power to decide on the cliffs which, in his opinion, form the natural boundaries of benches.

4. The gold commissioner may, in any mine of any denomination where the pay dirt is thin or claims in small demand, or where from any circumstance he shall deem it reasonable, allow any free miner to register two claims in his own name, and allow such period as he may think proper for non-working either one of such claims. But no person shall be entitled to hold at one time more than two claims of the legal size. A discoverer's claim shall for this purpose be reckoned as one ordinary claim.

5. All claims shall be subject to the public rights of way and water in such manner, direction, and extent as the gold commissioner shall from time to time direct; no mine shall be worked within ten feet of any road, unless by the previous sanction of the gold commissioner.

6. In order to ascertain the quantity of water in any ditch or sluice, the following rules shall be observed, viz.:—

The water taken into a ditch shall be measured at the ditch head. No water shall be taken into a ditch except in a trough whose top and floor shall be horizontal planes, and sides parallel vertical planes; such trough to be continued for six times its breadth in a horizontal direction from the point at which the water enters the trough. The top of the trough to be not more than seven inches, and the bottom of the trough not more than seventeen inches, below the surface of the water in the reservoir, all measurements being taken inside the trough and in the low-water or dry season. The area of a vertical transverse section of the trough shall be considered as the measure of the quantity of water taken by the ditch.

## II.

### THE LAW OF LAND SALES IN THE COLONIES.

1. That from and after the date hereof (January 4th, 1860), British subjects, and aliens who shall take the oath of allegiance to Her Majesty and her successors, may acquire unoccupied and unreserved and unsurveyed Crown land in British Columbia (not being the site of an existent or

proposed town, or auriferous land available for mining purposes, or an Indian Reserve or Settlement), in fee simple, under the following conditions.

2. The person desiring to acquire any particular plot of land of the character aforesaid, shall enter into possession thereof and record his claim to any quantity not exceeding 160 acres thereof, with the magistrate residing nearest thereto, paying to the said magistrate the sum of eight shillings for recording such claim. Such piece of land shall be of a rectangular form, and the shortest side of the rectangle shall be at least two-thirds of the longest side. The claimant shall give the best possible description thereof to the magistrate with whom his claim is recorded, together with a rough plan thereof, and identify the plot in question by placing at the corners of the land four posts, and by stating in his description any other landmarks on the said 160 acres which he may consider of a noticeable character.

3. Whenever the Government survey shall extend to the land claimed, the claimant who has recorded his claim as aforesaid, or his heirs, or in

case of the grant of certificate of improvement hereinafter mentioned, the assigns of such claimant, shall, if he or they shall have been in continuous occupation of the same land from the date of the record aforesaid, be entitled to purchase the land so pre-empted at such rate as may, for the time being, be fixed by the Government of British Columbia, not exceeding the sum of ten shillings per acre.*

4. No interest in any plot of land acquired as aforesaid, shall, before payment of the purchase money, be capable of passing to a purchaser unless the vendor shall have obtained a certificate from the nearest magistrate that he has made permanent improvements on the said plot to the value of ten shillings per acre.

5. Upon payment of the purchase money, a conveyance of the land purchased shall be executed in favour of the purchaser, reserving the precious minerals, with a right to enter and work the same in favour of the Crown, its assigns and licencees.

6. Priority of title shall be obtained by the per-

---

* The price of land in these colonies has recently been fixed at 4s. 2d. per acre.

son first in occupation, who shall first record his claim in manner aforesaid.

7. Any person authorized to acquire land under the provisions of this Proclamation, may purchase, in addition to the land pre-empted in manner aforesaid, any number of acres not otherwise appropriated, at such rate as may be fixed by the Government, at the time when such land shall come to be surveyed, not to exceed ten shillings per acre; five shillings to be paid down, and the residue at the time of survey.

8. In the event of the Crown, its assigns or licencees, availing itself, or themselves, of the reservation mentioned in clause 5, a reasonable compensation for the waste and damage done, shall be paid by the person entering and working, to the person whose land shall be wasted or damaged as aforesaid, and in case of dispute, the same shall be settled by a jury of six men, to be summoned by the nearest magistrate.

9. Whenever any person shall permanently cease to occupy land pre-empted as aforesaid, the magistrate resident nearest to the land in question may in a summary way, on being satisfied of such

permanent cessation, cancel the claim of the person so permanently ceasing to occupy the same, and record the claim thereto of any other person satisfying the requisitions aforesaid.

10. The decision of the magistrate may be appealed by either party to the decision of the Judge of the Supreme Court of Civil Justice of British Columbia.

11. Any person desirous of appealing in manner aforesaid, may be required, before such appeal be heard, to find such security as may be hereafter pointed out by the rules or orders hereinafter directed to be published.

12. The procedure before the magistrate and judge respectively, shall be according to such rules and orders as shall be published by such judge, with the approbation of the Governor for the time of British Columbia.

13. Whenever a person in occupation at the time of record aforesaid, and he, his heirs, or assigns, shall have continued in permanent occupation of land pre-empted, or of land purchased as aforesaid, he or they may, save as hereinafter mentioned, bring ejectment or trespass against any

intruder upon the land so pre-empted or purchased, to the same extent as if he or they were seised of the legal estate in possession in the land so pre-empted or purchased.

14. Nothing herein contained shall be construed as giving a right to any claimant to exclude free miners from searching for any of the precious minerals, or working the same upon the conditions aforesaid.

15. The Government shall, notwithstanding any claim, record, or conveyance aforesaid, be entitled to enter and take such portion of the land pre-empted or purchased as may be required for roads or other public purposes.

16. Water privileges and the right of carrying water for mining purposes, may, notwithstanding any claim recorded, purchase or conveyance, aforesaid, be claimed and taken upon, under or over the said land so pre-empted or purchased as aforesaid by free miners requiring the same, and obtaining a grant or licence from the gold commissioner, and paying a compensation for waste or damage to the person whose land may be wasted or damaged by such water privilege or carriage of water, to

be ascertained in case of dispute in manner aforesaid.

17. In case any dispute shall arise between persons with regard to any land so acquired as aforesaid, any one of the parties in difference may (before ejectment or action of trespass brought) refer the question in difference to the nearest magistrate, who is hereby authorized to proceed in a summary way to restore the possession of any land in dispute to the person whom he may deem entitled to the same, and to abate all intrusions, and award and levy such costs and damages as he may think fit.

Referring to the quantity, quality, and price of land, a correspondent of a local paper says:—
"The price of surveyed Crown land is 4s. 2d. sterling per acre—one half down, and the remainder in two years. Unsurveyed land can only be obtained by actual settlers. Any British subject can pre-empt 160 acres, and if he settle upon it in person or by proxy, he is allowed to purchase as much more in the same locality as he desires; and as soon as he makes improvements equal to two dollars and a half per acre of the whole he has located, he can get a certificate of title from

the resident magistrate, which is equal to a quit-claim deed. Then, so soon as he is prepared to pay for the survey of his land and one dollar per acre, he gets a regular Crown deed. Improvements that would be valued at 100 dols. in Canada would be reckoned at about 500 dols. here, and at 1,000 in the region of our gold fields."

## III.

ANNO VICESIMO PRIMO & VICESIMO SECUNDO.
VICTORIÆ REGINÆ.

CAP. XCIX.

AN ACT to provide for the Government of British Columbia.   [2d August, 1858.]
WHEREAS divers of Her Majesty's subjects and others have, by the licence and consent of Her Majesty, resorted to and settled on certain wild and unoccupied territories on the north-west coast of North America, commonly known by the designation of New Caledonia, and from and after the passing of this Act to be named British Columbia, and the islands adjacent for mining and other pur-

poses; and it is desirable to make temporary provision for the civil government of such territories, until permanent settlements shall be thereupon established, and the number of colonists increased: Be it therefore enacted by the Queen's most excellent Majesty, by and with the advice and consent of the Lords spiritual and temporal, and Commons, in this present Parliament assembled, and by the authority of the same, as follows:—

I. British Columbia shall, for the purposes of this Act, be held to comprise all such territories within the dominions of Her Majesty as are bounded to the south by the frontier of the United States of America,* to the east by the main chain of the Rocky Mountains, to the north by Simpson's River and the Finlay branch of the Peace River, and to the west by the Pacific Ocean, and shall include Queen Charlotte's Island, and all other islands adjacent to the said territories, except as hereinafter excepted.

II. It shall be lawful for Her Majesty, by any order or orders to be by her from time to time made, with the advice of her Privy Council, to

* The 49th Parallel of N. Latitude.

make, ordain, and establish, and (subject to such conditions or restrictions as to her shall seem meet) to authorize and empower such officer as she may from time to time appoint as Governor of British Columbia, to make provision for the administration of justice therein, and generally to make, ordain, and establish all such laws, institutions, and ordinances as may be necessary for the peace, order, and good government of Her Majesty's subjects and others therein; provided that all such Orders in Council, and all laws and ordinances so to be made as aforesaid, shall be laid before both Houses of Parliament as soon as conveniently may be after making and enactment thereof respectively.

III. Provided always, That it shall be lawful for Her Majesty, so soon as she may deem it convenient, by any such Order in Council as aforesaid, to constitute or to authorize and empower such officer to constitute a Legislature to make laws for the peace, order, and good government of British Columbia, such Legislature to consist of the Governor and a Council, or Council and Assembly, to be composed of such and so many persons, and to be appointed or elected in such manner and for such periods, and subject to such regulations, as to Her Majesty may seem expedient.

IV. And whereas an Act was passed in the forty-third year of King George the Third, intituled "An Act for Extending the Jurisdiction of the Courts of Justice in the Provinces of Lower and Upper Canada, to the trial and punishment of persons guilty of crimes and offences within certain parts of North America adjoining to the said Provinces: And whereas by an Act passed in the second year of King George the Fourth, intituled an Act for Regulating the Fur Trade, and Establishing a Criminal and Civil Jurisdiction within certain parts of North America, it was enacted, that from and after the passing of that Act the Courts of Judicature then existing or which might be thereafter established in the Province of Upper Canada should have the same civil jurisdiction, power and authority within the Indian territories and other parts of America not within the limits of either of the provinces of Lower or Upper Canada or of any civil government of the United States, as the said Courts had or were invested with within the limits of the said provinces of Lower or Upper Canada respectively, and that every contract, agreement, debt, liability and demand made, entered into, incurred, or arising within the said Indian territories and other parts of America, and every wrong and injury to the person or to property committed or done within the same, should be and be deemed to be of the same nature, and be cognizable and be tried in the same manner, and subject to the same consequences in all respects, as if the same had been made, entered into, incurred, arisen, committed or done within the said province of Upper Canada; and in the same Act are contained provisions for giving force, authority and effect within the said Indian territories and other parts of America to the process and acts of the said Courts of Upper Canada; and it was thereby also enacted, that it should be lawful for His Majesty, if he should deem it convenient so to do, to issue a commission or commissions to any person or persons to be and act as Justices of the Peace within such parts of America as aforesaid, as well within any territories theretofore granted to the company of adventurers of England trading to Hudson's Bay as within the Indian territories of such other parts of America as aforesaid; and it was further enacted, that it should be lawful for His Majesty from time to time by any commission under the Great Seal to authorize and empower any such persons so appointed Justices of the Peace as aforesaid to sit and hold Courts of Record for the trial of criminal offences and misdemeanours, and also of civil causes, and it should be lawful for His Majesty to order, direct and authorize the appointment of proper officers to act in aid of such courts and justices within the jurisdiction assigned to such courts and justices in any such commission; provided that such courts should not try any offender upon any charge or indictment for any felony made the subject of capital punishment, or for any offence or passing sentence affecting the life of any offender, or adjudge or cause any offender to suffer capital punishment or transportation, or take cognizance of or try any civil action or suit in which the cause of such suit or action should exceed in value the amount or sum of two hundred pounds, and in every case of any offence subjecting the person committing the same to capital punishment or transportation, the Court, or any Judge of any such Court, or any Justice or Justices of the Peace before whom any such offender should be brought, should commit such offender to safe custody, and cause such offender to be sent in such custody for trial in the Court of the province of Upper Canada.

From and after the proclamation of this Act in British Columbia the said Act of the forty-third year of King George the Third, and the said recited provisions of the said Act of the second year of King George the Fourth, and the provisions contained in such Act for giving force, authority and effect within the Indian territories and other parts of America to the process and acts of the said Courts of Upper Canada, shall cease to have force in and to be applicable to British Columbia.

V. Provided always, That all judgments given in any civil suit in British Columbia shall be subject to appeal to Her Majesty in Council, in the manner and subject to the regulations in and subject to which appeals are now brought from the Civil Courts of Canada, and to such further or other regulations as Her Majesty, with the advice of Her Privy Council, shall from time to time appoint.

VI. No part of the colony of Vancouver Island as at present established, shall be comprised within British Columbia for the purpose of this Act; but it shall be lawful for Her Majesty, her heirs and successors, on receiving at any time during the continuance of this Act a joint address from the two Houses of the Legislature of Vancouver Island, praying for the incorporation of that Island with British Columbia, by order to be made as aforesaid with the advice of her Privy Council, to annex the said island to British Columbia, subject to such conditions and regulations as to Her Majesty shall seem expedient; and thereupon and from the date of the publication of such order in the said Island, or such other date as may be fixed in such order, the provisions of this Act shall be held to apply to Vancouver Island.

VII. In the construction of this Act the term "Governor" shall mean the person for the time being lawfully administering the Government of British Columbia.

VIII. This Act shall continue in force until the thirty-first day of December, one thousand eight hundred and sixty-two, and thenceforth to the end of the then next session of Parliament; provided always, that the expiration of this Act shall not affect the boundaries hereby defined, or the right of appeal hereby given, or any act done or right or title acquired under or by virtue of this Act, nor shall the expiration of this Act revive the Acts or parts of Acts hereby repealed.

THE END.

www.ingramcontent.com/pod-product-compliance
Lightning Source LLC
Chambersburg PA
CBHW022024240426
43667CB00042B/1089